Boosting School Belonging

With rising rates of youth mental illness, disconnection and social isolation, strategies are needed that can help stem the tide. A sense of belonging to one's school is associated with good school performance, physical and psychological wellbeing, and offers a quintessential solution to help address many of the issues faced by young people today.

Grounded in theory, research, and practical experience, *Boosting School Belonging* provides 48 activities for practitioners and teachers to use with classes, groups, or individuals to help secondary students develop a sense of school belonging. Through six modules, readers will understand the evidence underlying each module, identify fun and practical tools to use with young people, and develop strategies for helping young people connect with teachers, parents, peers, themselves, learning, and help.

The evidence-based strategies and concepts make it an invaluable resource for teachers, psychologists and counsellors looking to help foster a sense of school belonging amongst students.

Dr Kelly-Ann Allen is an endorsed Educational and Developmental Psychologist, senior lecturer at Monash University and Fellow of the College of Educational and Developmental Psychologists. Dr Allen is also an honorary fellow of the Centre for Positive Psychology, Melbourne Graduate School of Education, the University of Melbourne. She is nationally and internationally recognised both as a researcher and practitioner in social connectedness, belonging, and social and emotional learning, and for her translation of this expertise within educational contexts as a consultant and school psychologist, and provides professional supervision to psychologists at different stages of career in private practice and schools. Dr Allen has contributed numerous publications and has presented at national and international conferences. Dr Allen's professional standing is verified by her full membership of the Australian Psychological Society and College of Educational and Developmental Psychologists, where she is currently treasurer of the national committee. You can find out more about Dr Allen's work at www.drkellyallen.com.

Dr Peggy (Margaret) Kern is an associate professor at the Centre for Positive Psychology at the University of Melbourne's Graduate School of Education. Dr Kern received her undergraduate degree in psychology from Arizona State University, a Masters and PhD in social/personality psychology from the University of California, Riverside, and postdoctoral training at the University of Pennsylvania. She has published two books and over 80 peer-reviewed articles and chapters. Her research is collaborative in nature and draws on a variety of methodologies to examine questions around who thrives in life and why, including: (a) understanding and measuring healthy functioning, (b) identifying individual and social factors impacting life trajectories, and (c) systems informed approaches to wellbeing. You can find out more about Dr Kern's work at www.peggykern.org.

Boosting School Belonging

Practical Strategies to Help Adolescents
Feel Like They Belong at School

Kelly-Ann Allen and Peggy Kern

Routledge
Taylor & Francis Group

LONDON AND NEW YORK

First published 2020
by Routledge
2 Park Square, Milton Park, Abingdon, Oxon OX14 4RN

and by Routledge
52 Vanderbilt Avenue, New York, NY 10017

Routledge is an imprint of the Taylor & Francis Group, an informa business

British Library Cataloguing-in-Publication Data
A catalogue record for this book is available from the British Library

Library of Congress Cataloging-in-Publication Data
Names: Allen, Kelly-Ann (Educational psychologist), author. |
    Kern, Peggy, 1980- author.
Title: Boosting school belonging : practical strategies to help
    adolescents feel like they belong at school / Kelly-Ann Allen
    and Peggy Kern.
Description: Abingdon, Oxon ; New York, NY : Routledge, 2019. |
    Includes bibliographical references and index.
Identifiers: LCCN 2019009053| ISBN 9781138305106 (hbk) |
    ISBN 9781138305083 (pbk) | ISBN 9780203729632 (ebk)
Subjects: LCSH: Belonging (Social psychology) | Adolescent
    psychology. | School environment. | Educational psychology. |
    Teacher-student relationships.
Classification: LCC LC210 .A44 2019 | DDC 370.15/8—dc23
LC record available at https://lccn.loc.gov/2019009053

ISBN: 978-1-138-30510-6 (hbk)
ISBN: 978-1-138-30508-3 (pbk)
ISBN: 978-0-203-72963-2 (ebk)

Typeset in Bembo
by Swales & Willis Ltd, Exeter, Devon, UK

Visit the eResources: https://www.routledge.com/9781138305083

For all those who felt like they never belonged in school and hope their children will not have to have the same experience.

Contents

5   Connecting with learning   117

6   Connecting with help   151

Foreword

It was with great delight that I accepted the invitation to write the foreword for this book. When Kelly Allen first approached me to supervise her PhD on school belonging, I asked her why she was interested in this topic. Kelly, a school psychologist, relayed a story to me of a middle-aged, homeless woman who had been parking her car outside of the school grounds and sleeping there each night. The police had to move this lady on several times because her car was disrupting the morning traffic. Feeling compassion for the women, and not wanting the police to have to intervene again, Kelly spoke to her about moving on and in the conversation asked her a seemingly simple question 'Why have you chosen this spot to sleep each night?' The woman replied that this was the school she had gone to as a kid and it was the one place where she felt she belonged. She returned to sleep there now because it made her remember happier times in her life. Kelly's simple question was met with a profound answer by the homeless women that kickstarted Kelly off on a journey to scientifically study the factors that promote school belonging.

The need to belong is a fundamental human need that, when not met, leads to a raft of unwanted consequences both physical and psychological. Social isolation is a health risk factor equal to or greater than that associated with smoking, obesity, or high blood pressure. Loneliness has become one of the major threats to the mental health of people across the globe.

The child and teen years are the life stage where we form our identity and school is the place where much of this transpires. A school that helps a young person belong and meet their social needs also reaps the benefits of having engaged students who do well academically and have strong mental health.

Kelly's PhD identified that belonging is not just a feeling with a student but is a social phenomenon that is created through the entire eco-system of a school. The current book, co-authored with Dr Peggy Kern, another of Kelly's PhD supervisors, does a sterling job of taking the ecological approach supported by science and creating concrete, practical actions and exercises that each member of the school community can put into action to foster a culture of belonging. It will no doubt be read and used widely across the globe.

Professor Lea Waters, PhD
Centre for Positive Psychology
Melbourne Graduate School of Education
The University of Melbourne

Preface

This book builds upon research that we completed at the University of Melbourne. The research clearly shows how important a sense of belonging is. Belonging has not only been linked to better mental health outcomes in adolescence, but it is also associated with better school performance, greater retention, and good long-term physical, mental, and social outcomes. Research has found that 1 in 4 adolescents report feeling disconnected from their school. This statistic represents international prevalence and demonstrates that school belonging needs to be critically addressed.

When I first began research related to my work as an educational and developmental psychologist, I never imagined that I would be writing anything other than peer-reviewed journal articles. But with a growing list of publications under my belt, I quickly became aware that the articles I was writing were not necessarily reaching the audience I had hoped for. I have worked in schools for a number of years and most of my colleagues were not paying for journal access. Our school libraries did not subscribe to academic databases and for those colleagues not studying at a university, access to a simple journal article was a challenge. While most people can see the tremendous benefit of accessing new research related to their vocational interests, most professionals working in education are not accessing the research that could benefit them and their students the most. It's no wonder that many writers describe the existence of a research-practice gap. Even for the field of school belonging, what is known in the literature is not necessarily translated in schools.

This book aims to bridge that gap. We present research-driven strategies and concepts concerned with school belonging to help educators and practitioners guide adolescents to connect with and stay at school.

The book is designed for practitioners and educators to foster a sense of belonging in adolescents, especially for those who work with adolescents aged 12–18 years. It can be used in an individual or group context and also as a therapeutic tool or a group/classroom preventative tool.

I hope that the chapters and modules empower educators and practitioners to help our young people grow their sense of affiliation to school and experience all of the associated benefits of feeling a sense of school belonging.

Dr Kelly-Ann Allen

Adolescent belonging is a topic close to my heart. Throughout my teenage years, I longed to feel a sense of belonging, but struggled to find it – I never felt like I really fit in. I still remember sixth grade. I had two girls that I called friends, but always felt more like the third wheel. Day after day I came home from school in tears, struggling with their passive aggression. My mum graciously comforted me, with her own heart probably breaking over watching me struggle. I threw myself into academics, working hard to be an A+ student, trying to somehow prove myself to others (or to myself) by showing I was "smart". Teachers liked me and my parents supported me, but I feared that their love was based on my performance. As the years passed by and I drifted in and out of different social groups. I became a high achiever, working long hours to earn high marks. But my mental health suffered.

The skills that we are teaching young people through positive education and social and emotional learning certainly would have changed my teenage experiences. Over the years, I learned to be socially adept, but it was a long learning process, with many struggles along the way. We are teaching young people how to be friends to others, how to support and be supported by others, how to connect with and care for oneself, and how to seek help when needed.

The strategies in this book are grounded in research and our own experience, but some will fit better than others. We encourage you to try things out, take the activities that you find useful, leave the ones that are less so. But keep working at it. Building a sense of belonging requires getting to know yourself, opening up to others, and caring about the needs of others. It takes time. But if even one student has a better teenage experience through our efforts, then it is well worth the time and effort given.

Dr Peggy Kern

Acknowledgements

A very special heartfelt thanks goes out to Professors Lea Waters and Dianne Vella-Brodrick from the Melbourne Graduate School of Education, The University of Melbourne. Both of these amazing, intelligent women had a significant hand to play in the development of the empirical research conducted that was the inspiration for writing this book. It is also with great gratitude and respect that we also thank Associate Professor Erica Frydenberg and Dr Vicki McKenzie for their ongoing support and mentoring. A special thanks to Heather Craig and Christine Marie Almanza for their input, ideas, and proof-reading. We acknowledge the wonderful contributions of Emma Cleine, who provided the cover art, and Kathryn Kallady, who helped us visualise our ideas captured within the rainbow model of school belonging. We are grateful for their skill, care in their work, and the resulting beautiful illustrations bringing a sense of belonging to life.

We would also both like to thank our mothers (Rose O'Brien and Barb Kern), who taught us what belonging meant from the moment that we were born. They showed us unconditional love and have been exemplary models of strong, independent, supportive women. We thank these amazing women for helping to shape who we are, taking interest in the work that we do, and for continually believing in and supporting us through the many highs and lows of life.

Introduction

Take a moment and think about your teenage years. What were they like? Perhaps a trip down memory lane brings back fond memories. A time when life was easy – you spent time with your best friends, had a crush on a cute boy or girl, and did just enough schoolwork to get by. Perhaps you played sports or an instrument. Or you challenged yourself academically, working hard to get top marks and to be accepted into your dream university or job.

Or perhaps secondary school is a time you would rather forget. A time of rejection. You felt self-conscious or thought you did not fit in. You dreaded each day as you tried to survive the cruelties of classmates, teachers, administrators, parents, and others.

We all have a need to belong. Educational communities are critical in either supporting and building or hindering and destroying a sense of belonging. And that's what this book is all about.

We begin with diving deeper into what school belonging is and why it matters. Subsequent chapters provide modules with strategies and hands-on activities to help you proactively support young people to develop a sense of belonging to their school.

Why school belonging?

When a young person describes connection with their school, it ranges along a continuum from a deep sense of connection and belonging to complete detachment and isolation. Those who work with youth – teachers, principals, social workers, psychologists, school nurses, and others – usually have witnessed a broad spectrum. There are those who are so patriotic to the school that they earn degrees specifically so they can return and teach at the school. Then there are the students who never show up – you do what you can to encourage them to connect, but it can be a challenge. Most students fall somewhere in between these two extremes.

Struggles with belonging can manifest in different ways. Some students present with concerns such as depression, anxiety, peer conflict, interpersonal difficulties with staff, disengagement with school work, or victimisation. Others engage in self-harm or disordered eating, or struggle completing classwork.

Still others bully others, abuse alcohol and other drugs. They may skip class, or if they do attend, do not pay attention to the material. At an extreme, they drop out or are expelled from school.

The onset of mental illness typically presents during adolescence, with a quarter of adolescents reporting symptoms of mental illness (Allen & McKenzie, 2015). Over 50% of illness reported by adolescents is attributed to mental illness. In Australia, suicide is the number one cause of death for young people aged between 15 and 24. These mental health statistics for young people are concerning.

The burden of mental illness does not only impact the adolescent; parents, families, teachers, peers, neighbours, and society as a whole also suffer. Parents want their child to be happy and feel helpless when their child struggles with mental health difficulties. Teachers are overwhelmed, with little training to deal with the mental health concerns that their students present. Too many students are grieving the loss of a friend due to suicide. And the financial burden on society, in terms of both treated and untreated medical care and lives prematurely lost or disabled, is astronomical.

The causes for such a mental illness burden are varied and complex. School belonging is not the only contributor, but certainly plays a role in adding risk or offering protection.

School belonging is positively associated with various academic outcomes, including educational motivation classroom engagement, improved school attendance, and academic performance (e.g., Anderman & Freeman, 2004; Croninger & Lee, 2001; Furlong et al., 2011; Goodenow & Grady, 1993; Klem & Connel, 2003; Resnick et al., 1997). It is positively associated with feeling satisfied with life, happiness, self-esteem, personal identity, friendships, acceptance, positive relationships with teachers and help seeking behaviours (Hamm & Faircloth, 2005; Nutbrown & Clough, 2009; Osterman, 2000). And it is negatively associated with various behaviours not conducive to school, including fighting, bullying, vandalism, absenteeism, school drop-out rates, disruptive behaviour, and substance and tobacco use (Connell et al., 1995; Croninger & Lee, 2001; Goodenow & Grady, 1993; Lonczak, Abbott, Hawkins, Kosterman & Catalano, 2002; Wilson & Elliot, 2003).

The research is clear. Students who feel a sense of belonging to school, pay more attention in class, do more than is expected of them by their teachers, and earn higher grades and scores. Second to home, school is the most important environment in the lives of young people. Feeling engaged at school is critical for both academic and social success.

Yet despite these benefits, many young people struggle to feel a sense of belonging. In 2015, the Programme for International Assessment Data (PISA) surveyed Australian students, asking them whether they agree or disagree with the statement, "I belong at school". 27% of students disagreed. Around the world, across 72 nations, PISA found a clear and consistent trend – many students feel like they don't belong at school. This is disconcerting, given that school is the place where teenagers spend many of their waking hours. In a society that is increasingly interconnected through various technologies, many young people feel alone and disconnected.

Schools are uniquely placed to proactively support youth at a time of high vulnerability. Adolescents are developing a sense of personal identity, trying to understand who they are and how they fit in the world. Young people spend a lot of time at school, and the dominance it plays in their lives impacts their thoughts, emotions, behaviours, and sense of self. With shifting societal structures, schools often are expected to address many of the psychological and social needs that previously were met at home. As such, proactively supporting the wellbeing and mental health of all students should be a priority. School leaders and professionals should have a clear understanding of the importance a student's sense of school belonging plays in respect to wellbeing and mental health. This book endeavours to facilitate this understanding and to provide practical interventions to help each secondary school student to feel like they belong.

What is school belonging?

What do we mean when we talk about school belonging? Thinking back to your high school years, to what extent would you agree with the following statements?

- I feel like a part of my school.
- I feel proud to belong to my school.
- Most teachers at my school are interested in me.
- I am included in a lot of activities at my school.
- I can really be myself at my school.

These are some of the questions that are commonly used to assess school belonging (Goodenow & Grady, 1993)

In the research, school belonging is described using a range of terms such as:

- school bonding.
- school climate.
- notions of territory.
- school attachment.
- connectedness to school.
- student engagement.
- school membership.

Not belonging is also described using a range of terms:

- alienated
- ostracized
- disengaged

- socially isolated
- disaffected.

The different terms are also defined and used in various ways. The various terms and definitions used can make it hard for researchers to make sense of the literature – let alone educators and practitioners. Fortunately, over the past several years, we have diligently worked to bring order to this literature, both in terms of dissecting what the research has found, as well as thinking about and trying out ways to bring the research to life. As this book is focused more on practical application, we offer just a taste of the research here. If you want to learn more about school belonging, check out our book: *School Belonging in Adolescents: Theory, Research, and Practice* (Allen & Kern, 2017).

Perhaps the most commonly used definition was offered by Goodenow and Grady (1993): "the extent to which students feel personally accepted, respected, included, and supported by others in the school social environment" (p. 80). As this is one of the most commonly cited definitions of school belonging in the literature, it's the definition that we will used to define school belonging throughout this book.

Breaking this definition down further, we see several characteristics.

- It is a *feeling*. It's not about how many "friends" a student might have on social media or the number of clubs they are involved in, but rather a subjective sense that others actually care about them, accept them, and respect them, as they are.
- It's *personal*. The student is known by others – not just by name or face, but others know their interests, fears, hopes, and dreams.
- The student is *accepted*, for who they are, both their strengths and weaknesses.
- They are *respected* by others, treated with a full sense of humanity, no matter their background or ways that they might be different.
- They are *included* – an active part of the community, involved in class activities, social groups, clubs, sports team, drama, choir, debate team, or other parts of the school community.
- And they are *supported*, able to get help when needed, be it with schoolwork, emotional or social concerns, problems at home, or other concerns, large or small.
- Finally, all of this is enabled *by others in the school community*. It takes a village to raise a child, and it takes a school community to create a sense of belonging – peers, teachers, parents, staff, and school leaders all play a role in making each student feel like he or she belongs.

Teachers are a critical part of this. Studies clearly shows that positive student–teacher relationships have the greatest impact on school belonging. Students are more likely to report feeling like they belong when they sense that one or more teachers care about their learning, have an interest in them as individuals, and have high academic expectations.

Figure 0.1 All members of a school community are innately connected through
multiple layers and systems that operate within a school.

While teachers play a critical role, others in the school community matter
as well. All members of a school community are innately connected through
multiple layers and systems that operate within a school. For example, when
Kelly was a school psychologist, it was rare that Kelly would treat a student in
complete isolation. Within the limits of confidentiality, often there is a need
to consult with peers, teachers, parents, policies, practices, or local agencies to
influence the best outcome for the student.

A multi-systemic approach to belonging

Our research highlighted that various models have been used to understand
and explain a sense of belonging. Some focus on personal characteristics of
students, identify what distinguishes the connected and disconnected. Others
have focused on social relationships, including the influence of teachers, parents, and peers. And still others focus on the school climate; the physical environment, identifying steps schools, communities, and public policy can take to
create supportive, inclusive environments.

While these different models and frameworks can be useful for understanding what belonging is, why it matters, why belonging matters, and what
impacts belonging, what is needed is a *multi-systemic approach* in order to foster
belonging. The school community is an interconnected system. Every student,

teacher, staff member, leader, and parent play a role in creating a community that each member can feel a part of.

What do we mean by multi-systemic? A system is a set of people or things that are interconnected in such a way that they create unique patterns over time (Meadows, 2008). Systems range from very small (e.g., the human body), to very large (e.g., the solar system). What are some of the systems occurring within a school?

- **A student's individual factors**. Each student is a unique individual who has individual needs and experiences school in their own way, based on their prior experiences, perception of those experiences, thoughts, feelings, beliefs, social and emotional competencies, personality, mental health and temperament, biology, developmental considerations, social identity, and other individual characteristics (such as their academic motivation towards school). This means that two students, at the same school, can report completely different feelings towards the school.
- **Primary social groups**. Include members of family, friends, peers, teachers, and social groups. Some individuals have more influence than others – and the impact differs for each student. Each relationship can be a positive or negative influence on school belonging. For example, parental attitudes towards school and education can influence feelings of belonging to school. The relationships that a student has with the groups and individuals listed above is also important.
- **The school climate and physical environment.** This includes organisational structures, school culture and policies – the ways that the school operates and the social and physical environment that it creates for students and staff. It includes interactions amongst students, staff, leadership, parents, and others in the educational community. It also includes physical spaces within the school that allow for social inclusion, play and opportunities to form groups.
- **The local village**. This includes interactions with neighbours, local shopkeepers, general practitioners, support people (e.g., psychologists, social workers), and others in the community also including online communities. Depending on the nature of relationships in this group, some members can also fall into the primary social groups system.
- **Environs.** This refers to the local environment surrounding the student, and includes the physical space and community (e.g., rural, urban; communal or separated, physical safety).
- **The culture.** These are broader cultural factors, including cultural heritage and identity, ethnicity, religion, policies, and economic factors. This includes government driven priorities and legislation, media, and the shifting needs of society. This might be local, national, or international.
- **The ecosystem.** This is the earth and land on which we dwell. For instance, lack of care of the environment has led to natural disasters, climate change, and pollution, which filter down to affect the health and wellbeing of the people within that environment.

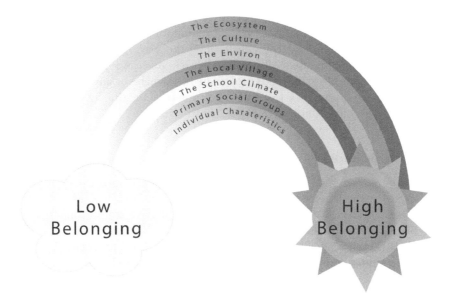

Figure 0.2 The Rainbow Model of School Belonging, which shows the multiple layers of influences on a student's sense of school belonging.

This may seem complex, but the key is to recognise the complexity but then pick small, simple places to intervene. That is, where can we make the biggest difference with the least amount of effort? We use a Rainbow Model of School Belonging to represent the different systems concerned with school belonging (Figure 0.2; a full colour copy of this module can be downloaded from https://www.routledge.com/9781138305083).

The Rainbow Model of School Belonging

The Rainbow Model of School Belonging visually captures the seven systems concerned with school belonging: a student's individual characteristics, primary social groups, the school climate, the local village, the environ, the culture, and the ecosystem.

The rainbow is a spectrum of colours – like the spectrum of belonging. The different layers might be brighter or lighter, depending on how much influence that layer has. Some days these feelings can be more intense than others, and the rainbow captures the range from rainclouds (low sense of belonging) to bright sunshine (high sense of belonging). Experiences of belonging to school are unique to the individual – just like each rainbow is unique (e.g., different sizes, times, and places).

On special days, a double rainbow appears – one being the reflection of the other. The inside becomes the outside. Likewise, each system comprises bidirectional influences.

Belonging to school can also be conceived as the ultimate pot of gold under the rainbow. School belonging is positively associated with a range of good outcomes for students that last well into adulthood. While challenges and stressors will occur for the individual along the way, we present activities and ideas to overcome these obstacles. After all, you can't have the rainbow without the rain. Helping health professionals, teachers, or anybody working with students to boost a sense of school belonging for the student in their care, is the impetus for writing this book.

About this book

In this book, we build upon empirical research that we conducted with our colleagues at the University of Melbourne. Based on a very extensive review, that research identified ten different themes that all have at least some impact on belonging (see Allen, Vella-Brodrick, & Waters, 2016, Allen, Kern, Vella-Brodrick, Hattie & Waters, 2018, and Allen & Kern, 2017 for details).

These studies provide insights into specific individual and social aspects that will benefit a student's sense of belonging the most – places for school leaders, teachers and practitioners to potentially intervene to help students feel more connected to their school. But the studies didn't show *how* to foster belonging. And that's what we do here.

Specifically, we focus on individual students and primary social groups, and the interconnections between them. This is not to say that schools should not be mindful of the broader systems at work, but for our purposes here, we focus on the areas that can be easily targeted by school professionals, mental health practitioners, and school leaders.

The proceeding chapters provide as series of modules that unpack different individual and social factors. Each one includes:

- a case study story that highlights the importance of the module
- a brief look at the research
- aims and objectives of the activity
- a detailed set of activities, with a final set of group or individual reflection questions.

The activities are designed for adolescents aged between 10 and 16 years. Most are suitable for working with groups/ classes or individual students. With professional discretion, the activities can be adapted to work with a broad range of student needs.

Module 1: Connecting with teachers

This module aims to encourage adolescents to use the support from teachers to assist with their connectedness to school. We discuss the importance of a positive student–teacher relationship (promoting mutual respect, care,

Figure 0.3 Module topics that relate to school belonging.

encouragement, friendliness, fairness, and autonomy). We provide strategies to help young people to actively develop a positive relationship with their teacher, perceive their teachers as likeable, accept their support (academic and personal) and foster a greater connection.

Module 2: Connecting with parents

This module discusses the role of family relationships in providing academic as well as social support, open communication, and supportive behaviour (e.g., accenting encouragement, gratitude). We discuss family engagement and ability to show care and compassion. We provide strategies that foster family connectedness (e.g., having fun together, paying attention to each other, feeling close, and listening skills).

Module 3: Connecting with peers

This module presents strategies for developing stronger relationships with peers. We identify strategies for building a sense of trust and provide ideas on how adolescents can become supportive peers themselves, providing social as well as academic encouragement to their friends and classmates. We discuss ways in which adolescents can show care and acceptance of others and build strong relationship skills.

Module 4: Connecting with oneself

While the prior modules focus on social relationships, this module turns to the individual student. The module aims to foster social and emotional competencies through a series of activities and self-reflection exercises. We include activities for developing self-efficacy, conscientiousness, coping skills (i.e., seeking social support, self-reliance, problem solving), positive affect, hope and hopefulness, school adjustment (i.e., making friends, staying out of trouble, getting along with teachers and students), and a sense of relatedness to others.

Module 5: Connecting with learning

Connecting learning with school belonging, this module focuses on academic motivation. Motivation towards learning is defined as the expectancy of academic success through goal setting and future aspirations. Academic motivation and school belonging are mutually enforcing of one another, so by helping a student's academic self-regulation, academic confidence, participation, motivation, and performance, not only assists academic performance, but also helps foster a love of learning and a sense of connection to places of learning (the school). We target planning, goal setting, and building academic confidence.

Module 6: Connecting with help

The other modules of this book aim to proactively develop mindsets, attitudes, behaviours, and competencies to help students feel a sense of connection to school and others. But school can still be a challenging place. Importantly, students don't need to deal with personal challenges alone. Students benefit from connecting with groups and systems around them – both the social systems such as peers, teachers, and parents, but also broader aspects of the school. This module provides accessible information on mental health. We normalise experiences related to mood regulation in adolescents, promote a preventative framework for mental illness, and list relevant help seeking resources.

We also emphasise the importance of considering the broader structures within a school (e.g., school priorities, policies, practices, school climate, school culture), and how these might assist or block students from seeking help as needed. By removing barriers and emphasising enablers, students will feel more supported and connected.

How to use the modules

The modules of this book can be used flexibly, dipping in and out of the modules or proceeding systematically through each one from start to finish. Each module can be used as a resource for working with groups (e.g., small groups or classes) or it can be used within a therapeutic context or more general work with individuals.

You might consider focusing on whichever areas students are struggling with. Appendix A provides a School Belonging Scale that students can complete (printable handouts and an online version are available at https://www.

routledge.com/9781138305083). While it can take some time (approx. 15 minutes), it can provide some good foundational information on how students are tracking – highlighting areas where they are doing well and areas where they are struggling.

Each student has the right to feel a sense of school belonging. While what we offer here cannot change every young person's experience at school, we hope these modules can help bridge the research between what scientists know and everyday practice. Even if a few students benefit, then it is well worth the effort.

References

Allen, K. & Kern, M. L. (2017). *School Belonging in Adolescents: Theory, research, and practice*. Singapore: Springer Social Sciences.

Allen, K., Kern, P., Vella-Brodrick, D., Hattie, J. & Waters, L. (2018). What schools need to know about belonging: A meta-analysis. *Educational Psychology Review*, *30*(1), 1–34. doi: 10.1007/s10648-016-9389-8

Allen, K. & McKenzie, V. (2015). Adolescent mental health in an Australian context and future interventions. *Special Issue on Mental Health in Australia for the International Journal of Mental Health*, *44*, 80–93. doi: 10.1080/00207411.2015

Allen, K., Vella-Brodrick, D., & Waters, L. (2016). Fostering school belonging in secondary schools using a socio-ecological framework. *The Educational and Developmental Psychologist*, *33*(1), 97–121. doi: 10.1017/edp.2016.5

Anderman, L. H., & Freeman, T. (2004). Students' sense of belonging in school. In M. L. Maehr & P. R. Pintrich (Eds), *Advances in motivation and achievement, volume 13: Motivating students, improving schools: The legacy of Carol Midgley* (pp. 27–63). Oxford, United Kingdom: Elsevier.

Connell, J. P., Halpern-Felsher, B., Clifford, E., Crichlow, W., & Usinger, P. (1995). Hanging in there: Behavioral, psychological, and contextual factors affecting whether African-American adolescents stay in school. *Journal of Adolescent Research*, *10*(1), 41–63.

Croninger, R. G., & Lee, V. E. (2001). Social capital and dropping out of high school: Benefits to at-risk students of teachers' support and guidance. *Teachers College Record*, *103*(4), 548–581.

Furlong, M. J., O'Brennan, L. M., & You, S. (2011). Psychometric properties of the Add Health School Connectedness Scale for 18 sociocultural groups. *Psychology in the Schools*, *48*(10), 986–997.

Goodenow, C., & Grady, K. E. (1993). The relationship of school belonging and friends' values to academic motivation among urban adolescent students. *Journal of Experimental Education*, *62*(1), 60–71.

Hamm, J. V., & Faircloth, B. S. (2005). The role of friendship in adolescents' sense of school belonging. *New Directions for Child and Adolescent Development*, *2005*(107), 61–78. doi: 10.1002/cd.121

Klem, A. M., & Connell, J. P. (2003, June). *Relationships matter: Linking teacher support to student engagement and achievement*. Paper presented at the Wingspread Conference on School Connectedness, Racine, WI.

Lonczak, H. S., Abbott, R. D., Hawkins, J. D., Kosterman, R., & Catalano, R. (2002). The effects of the Seattle social development project: Behavior, pregnancy, birth, and sexually transmitted disease outcomes by age 21. *Archives of Pediatric Adolescent Medicine, 156*, 438–447.

Meadows, D. H. (2008). *Thinking in systems: A primer.* White River Junction, VT: Chelsea Green Publishing.

Nutbrown, C., & Clough, P. (2009). Citizenship and inclusion in the early years: Understanding and responding to children's perspectives on 'belonging.' *International Journal of Early Years Education, 17*(3), 191–206. doi: 10.1080/09669760903424523

Osterman, K. F. (2000). Students' need for belonging in the school community. *Review of Educational Research, 70*(3), 323–367.

Resnick, M. D., Bearman, P. S., Blum, R. W., Bauman, K. E., Harris, K. M., Jones, J., . . . Uldry, J. R. (1997). Protecting adolescents from harm: Findings from the National Longitudinal Study on Adolescent Health. *Journal of the American Medical Association, 278*(10), 823–832.

Wilson, D., & Elliott, D. (2003, June). *The interface of school climate and school connectedness: An exploratory review and study.* Paper presented at the Wingspread Conference on School Connectedness, Racine, WI.

1 Connecting with teachers

The biggest influence on the connection you have to school is based on the teachers you have.
~ *Teagan, age 17*

Module at a glance

In brief

This module discusses the importance of the student–teacher relationship to a student's success and provides strategies to encourage positive relationships through different activities.

Learning outcomes

- Explain the challenges involved in connecting with teachers.
- Recognise the importance of building rapport between students and teachers.
- Identify and apply the strategies to develop positive student–teacher relationships.

Contents

A case study: Justine and Mrs Boss

Justine stormed into the school psychologist's office with confidence and sass that could only transpire from strong familiarity and years of developing rapport. The school psychologist had seen Justine on and off since Year 3, when she was referred for difficulties with inattention and organisational skills in the classroom, which later transpired to a diagnosis of ADHD (attention deficit hyperactivity disorder). Now in Year 10, Justine felt very comfortable with the school psychologist and freely came to her with difficulties.

"She hates me!" she exclaimed. The school psychologist knew instantly who she was talking about.

Since the school year started, Justine had been convinced that Mrs Boss, her accounting teacher, has it in for her. She believed that Mrs Boss chose favourites and she was not one of them. According to the school psychologist, this teacher frequently singles her out for not completing homework, not attending class on time, or not bringing the required materials to each lesson. "She gives me the evil eye," Justine would remark and, "she marks me lower than the others".

It was true that Justine's marks were much lower in this class when compared to her other subjects and her marks had dwindled for accounting throughout the year. Her report card reflected some concerns. Her teacher stated she was, "disorganised, inattentive, and easily distracted," which were difficulties Justine faced due to her diagnosis of ADHD. Statements such as these make us wonder whether teachers would make such obvious remarks in the report cards of students with physical difficulties (e.g., she has trouble walking, she is unable to hold a pencil correctly). Ultimately, the report card demonstrated that the teacher had strong opinions about Justine and failed to understand her. The rapport between Justine and Mrs Boss was non-existent and as a result, for a charismatic student like Justine who is driven by social interactions and pleasing others, both the student–teacher relationship and her marks in the class flailed.

Over the next few months, Justine's complaints continued. She finally provided the school psychologist with consent to talk to Mrs Boss directly. During the meeting, the school psychologist reminded the teacher about Justine's diagnosis of ADHD and what implications that may have on her learning and presentation in class. She was also able to emphasise the importance of developing a good rapport with Justine, as she had personally found that this paved the way for more cooperative interactions in a therapeutic context. Mrs Boss was surprised that Justine felt that she was disliked and with that information took steps to build their relationship through getting to know Justine more on a personal level (e.g., what are her hobbies, interests, and passions) and offering to be available to help Justine when she needed with her work.

It takes two to develop a relationship and, as a result, Justine had some personal work to do as well. The school psychologist worked with Justine to help her find things she liked about Mrs Boss and ensure she was using helpful language when describing their interactions. For example, "she always yells at me," was simply a distorted perspective that required challenging and reframing into a more realistic representation of their communication. Justine needed to look for the positive interactions she experienced rather than focusing on the negative ones.

As the year continued, Justine's marks for accounting improved dramatically. She developed an alliance with Mrs Boss that saw them mutually share goals related to Justine's success in the class. Justine shifted to believing that her teacher was there for her when she needed academic support, and even began confiding in Mrs Boss when she had other personal difficulties in her life. This paved the way for more empathy and understanding from Mrs Boss, who could see Justine as a student who needed a collaborative and supportive relationship to succeed. While Justine's inattention and disorganisation continued, Mrs Boss was able to focus on elements of Justine's approach to learning that could be changed (e.g., her effort) and this made things less frustrating for both of them.

What the research says

John Hattie (2009) tells us that the student–teacher relationship is fundamental to a student's success at school. His research shows that a positive student–teacher relationship can markedly bolster academic outcomes. Is this also true for school belonging?

As we dug into the research on this question, we were surprised to find how many relevant studies have been published (Allen, Kern, Vella-Brodrick, Waters, & Hattie, 2018). We found that the student–teacher relationship appears to be a more powerful influencer on belonging than relationships with peers or parents. For example, surveying 699 secondary school students, although parent support was indeed important for school belonging, teacher support mattered more. In fact, it had the largest effect size compared to any other factor we analysed. Hundreds of studies clearly indicate that having a positive relationship with at least one teacher (that is, the adolescent believes that their teacher is caring, empathic, fair, and able to help them resolve personal problems) is a foundation part of school belonging.

Like we saw with Justine, the quality of the student–teacher relationship depends in part on how much they prioritise creating a positive relationship. In a study with 115 students with disabilities, Crouch, Keys, and McMahon (2014) found that school belonging was lower for students who perceived their relationship with their teachers as negative, and higher in students who reported a positive relationship with their teacher. Interestingly, teacher and student ratings on the student's belonging were consistent. The extent to which this applies to students without disabilities is unclear but suggests that even though belonging is a subjective feeling, it shows up externally in ways that an observer teacher can see.

Although a teacher's primary role may be to teach certain material, their role extends far beyond providing opportunities for academic success. Teachers care about the development of the child as a whole, not just mastery of specific information. Cemalcilar (2010) found that teachers who respected and valued students, offered social support, and developed good rapport with their students were able to fulfil an important social function for students in addition to simply just delivering the curriculum. Students need to feel that their teachers respect them, care for them, and interact positively with them.

For many teachers, this may sound obvious and intuitive. But the reality is that even though teachers have good intentions, pressure from parents, school leaders, and school boards for high standardised test scores, combined with a crowded curriculum and large class sizes, result in little time for teachers to build important relationships with students and get to know them on a personal level. Governments and schools can place tremendous pressure on teachers through performance monitoring and grade-based priorities to increase the academic outcomes of students. Schools can spend a significant amount of time investing in professional development, and policies that aim to increase grades for students. Parents are often convinced that their son or daughter is a top student and needs to get into the best university. They can blame the school or teacher when their child fails to earn top marks.

But interestingly, the research shows that a teacher's ability to bolster study scores contributes little to a sense of belonging (Allen & Kern, 2017). Students want to know their teacher cares about them – even if they don't perform well. Indeed, lack of care can even undermine academic performance.

The research also shows that a teacher's wellbeing has a marked influence on the wellbeing of their students. The high academic pressures combined with trying to manage behavioural and personal issues of their students can take a toll. Teacher stress and burnout is widespread. Large portions of teachers are quitting within the first five years of graduating, despite the many years spent preparing to teach, the costs of that education, and the costs to the school in recruiting and training new teachers.

As a whole, we know that school belonging, a sense of wellbeing, and other psychosocial aspects of the student contribute to good mental health, lower the risk of suicide and suicide ideation, *and* increase academic performance.

In sum, schools must not underestimate the value and importance of the student–teacher relationship. It may seem that this relationship almost happens vicariously – simply by the student turning up to class each lesson, but in reality, like any other type of relationship, it takes effort and work.

School policy makers and leaders ought to reconsider how teachers are allocated time to build good relationships with their students. They might consider the increasing pressures on teachers to increase academic outcomes and how this may impact wellbeing for members of the school community. But we can't necessarily change governments and schools to prioritise academic outcomes over others that seemingly have just as much importance. So here we focus on what educators *can* do. Teachers matter, and fostering good student–teacher relationships is something that teachers and practitioners can do something about. And that's what this module is all about.

Module overview

This module aims to assist teachers and clinicians working with adolescents to build positive student–teacher relationships within their school. The activities herein provide strategies for a young person to actively build positive relationships with their teachers, perceive their teachers as likeable, and accept them for academic and personal support.

Before beginning, you might have students complete the Classroom Belonging Scale (see Appendix B; for an online version or paper handouts, see https://www.routledge.com/9781138305083), which allows each student to reflect on their own sense of belonging and can provide a classroom teacher with an indication of how the students are traveling. It can also be helpful for teachers to reflect on their own practices, providing an understanding of how the students see them from their perspectives. We then provide eight activities to help students better appreciate their teachers and consider what they can do to proactively build good relationships with their teachers. The module ends with a set of reflection questions, which might be used within a group discussion or for students to reflect on their own at a later time.

If you are working with a group or class of students, be mindful about the context in which the session is being held, the possible needs of the students, and limits of confidentiality. Students should be encouraged to treat one another with respect. It can be useful to remind students about the importance of treating others as they would like to be treated (e.g., "You wouldn't want others to go around school saying mean things about you, so it's important that you don't do this about others. What happens here needs to stay in this classroom.")

Activity 1: Getting to know you

Purpose: To get to know students better and illustrate the inter-connectedness of each member of the group or class.

Materials: Ball of string.

Suggested time for completion: 20–30 minutes.

Introduction

This activity allows students to get to know each other better and allows you to learn more about the students you are working with. Each person is asked to share an unusual or funny fact about themselves. Listen carefully. What the students decide to share (or not share) offers insights into who they are (their personality and temperament) and their comfort level within a group.

Instructions

Have students stand in a circle. Begin by sharing something about yourself – the stranger the better, as this invites students to be creative. Holding the end of the string, toss the ball to a student, and invite them share an unusual or funny fact about themselves. They hold the string and toss the ball to the next student, skipping around until all have shared. At the end, comment that each student has their own unique story, but we are all interconnected in various ways, and as such we need to look out for and support one another.

An added challenge

If time allows, have each student share three fun "facts", two that are true and one that is a lie. Other students vote on which is the lie, then the student indicates which two are correct.

Activity 2: The overgeneralising cheat sheet

Purpose: To identify and challenge distorted beliefs.

Materials: The *Overgeneralisation cheat sheet* worksheet (below; printable sheets available at https://www.routledge.com/9781138305083).

Suggested time for completion: 30–60 minutes.

Introduction

"She hates me."
"She always yells at me."
"She picks on me, I swear."
"She likes everybody else, but not me."
"She never chooses me."

Have you ever heard a student talk this way about a teacher? For psychologists, school counsellors, and other mental health professionals working in schools, these are phrases that are regularly heard. In reality, teachers usually don't dislike a student so strongly that it would warrant such negative beliefs held by a student (of course, there are exceptions). Yet no matter how inaccurate the statements may be, the perceptions are very real to the students themselves.

Psychologists call these strong misbeliefs "cognitive distortions". Cognitive distortions represent faulty or dysfunctional thinking that is inaccurate and largely irrational. There are various distortions that a person might make, such as *filtering* (only seeing the bad things that happen and not the good), *black and white thinking* (I'm either good or bad, smart or stupid), and *catastrophising* (assuming that the worst-case scenario will occur). The statements above represent *overgeneralisations*. Students who overgeneralise use words like "always", "never", and "every".

Cognitive distortions develop over time, often not appearing to others until the belief has become deeply ingrained. It might have begun from an isolated incident that triggered the student to feel insecure. Perhaps the teacher made an offhand comment or snide remark. As adolescents are forming a sense of identity, they may be particularly attuned to negative signals from others, which affirm and strengthen the initial belief. Over time, the distorted belief develops into broad and sweeping conclusions about the current state of their relationship with their teacher.

The thoughts manifest as intense negative emotions and behavioural problems. A student who perceives their teacher hates them, may feel frustrated, upset, annoyed, or distressed. He or she may skip class, act out, further sabotage the relationship with the teacher, be inattentive in class, or give little effort to classwork and homework.

Very distorted beliefs take a lot of time and effort to change, usually requiring work with a psychologist. But students (and the student–teacher relationship) can benefit from identifying distorted beliefs early on and learning to challenge and shift those beliefs before they become overwhelming and all-encompassing.

Notably, we all have distorted thoughts at different points in time, as we make assumptions about what other people are thinking, saying, feeling, or doing. Teachers too can benefit from taking time to identify what their beliefs are, and whether some of those beliefs might be distortions of the truth.

This activity comes from Cognitive Behavioural Therapy (CBT). It aims to help students identify overgeneralisations that they make, to challenge the distorted belief, and to consider whether a different belief would be more helpful.

This activity is particularly well suited for working directly with individual students thinking about another teacher but can also be useful in groups. In a group, it's important to be sensitive to students who might be struggling with the activity, checking in on individual students and referring on for additional care as needed.

It's important to note that there are cases where searching for additional evidence actually *does* support the negative belief rather than the alternative explanations. For instance, when teachers do display dislike toward a student, this activity may bring out more evidence for the negative thought. Such cases need to be dealt with carefully, first validating the feelings of the student, and then reaching out to others (e.g., school leadership, school psychologist, other teachers) to identify the problem and work together to provide support for both the student and teacher concerned – whether it is in the way of managing behaviours displayed by the student or in the case of needing to provide the teacher with professional development.

Instructions

Provide the student with the *Overgeneralisation cheat sheet* worksheet below (see overgeneralisations for printable handouts).

It can be challenging for some students to identify their distorted thinking and alternative explanations, especially if the distorted belief is strong. You might have the student complete the sheet, then discuss their answers with them, seeing if they were able to identify times that they overgeneralise and to challenge their faulty thinking. It can be useful to ask questions to generate thought, such as:

> Tell me about a time this week where you felt that your teacher did not like you. What happened? What did you think? How did you feel? What did you do? Were you able to challenge this thought? Did this have an impact on your feelings or behaviour? What else can we do to address this issue?

If needed, you can help think of alternative explanations, brainstorming ideas with the student.

If you are working with a class, this activity can be used to help students think about some of their beliefs and different explanations for this. Before handing out the worksheets, give an example of a distorted belief, along with several alternative explanations. Have the students complete the first two sections (beliefs and explanations). Next, with a partner or in small groups, have the students brainstorm other alternative explanations.

If students feel comfortable, they might discuss their actual beliefs and others can help identify alternatives. If they don't feel comfortable, then have them think about a hypothetical belief, and generate some alternative explanations together as a group. End with a brief discussion about how our thoughts can negatively impact us, and challenge students to keep challenging negative beliefs.

The overgeneralisation cheat sheet

Do you ever find yourself thinking things like "I *always* stuff things up", "my teacher likes *everyone* but me", or "I'll *never* learn this"? Statements such as "always", "everyone but me", and "never" are called *overgeneralisations*. While it may *seem* true, it is not *actually* true. Overgeneralisations are a type of faulty thinking. Overgeneralisations can have a negative impact on your relationships with others and make school are hard experience.

There may be some very good reasons why you believe what you do. Indeed, our brains are wired to find the negative in different situations. By being tuned into negative things, it can help protect us from danger. But the problem is when we see things as dangerous and threatening when in reality there are no dangers there.

Overgeneralising is easy to do and hard to stop – in part because we often don't realise that we are overgeneralising. The trick it to be able to identify when you are making an overgeneralisation, and to start challenging faulty thinking. This activity is meant to do just that.

First, think about something bad that you expect to happen over and over again.

What is your thought? _____

How does this thought make you feel?_____

On a scale of 0 (none) to 10 (overwhelming), how strong is this feeling?

_____

How does this feeling affect you at school? _____

_____

The next step is to challenge your thinking and consider whether a different thought may be more helpful.

What evidence do you have for this thought? _____

_____

If you were to share this thought with others, what would others say?

_____

_____

Are words like "always" and "never" accurate? Are there times when this is not true?

_____

What would be a more helpful thought? _____

_____

How would this alternative thought make you feel? _____

What might be evidence for this alternative thought? _____

_____

Now it's time to test out the new thought. Over the next few days, be an investigator. Talk to others. Hunt for evidence for the negative thought, and evidence for alternative explanations. For example, maybe you feel like your teacher hates you. Some alternative explanations might be that the teacher is really busy, and though they care, they are also trying to keep the class on track. The teacher is a human being and as a consequence displays a range of moods – it's not about me personally. **Find as much evidence as you can. Then return here and complete the remaining questions.**

What evidence did you find for the negative thought? _____

_____

_____

What evidence did you find for alternative explanations? _____

_____

_____

What do you believe now? _____

How does that make you feel? _____

Activity 3: Good vibes

Purpose: To develop a more balanced perception about the teacher or a person they dislike.

Materials: *Good vibes* handout (below and available at https://www.routledge.com/9781138305083).

Suggested time for completion: 20–30 minutes.

Introduction

When a student has a strong dislike of another person, particularly a teacher, it can create a roadblock in the relationship. This can make it challenging, both for the student and the teacher. Even as that teacher might make efforts to connect with the student, it can be like smacking into a wall and getting nowhere. The student sees everything the teacher does as negative or bad.

This activity is designed to provide an outlet for the student to describe all the things they dislike about a teacher and then refocus their thoughts on likeable characteristics. The activity aims to help students develop a more balanced perspective of their teacher and to recognise that while some people may have undesirable characteristics or traits, that most people are not *all bad* and that there may be some aspects to a person that are also good qualities.

Instructions

Introduce the activity by noting:

> There are some people who really get under our skin. You really dislike them, and they make life miserable for you. While some of the things the person does that annoys you are true, they also have some good aspects. Nobody is *all* bad. This might be one of your teachers, a peer, or someone else. This activity challenges you to consider what you dislike about the person – but also what some of their good parts might be.
>
> Take a few minutes and note the things you dislike about the person in the left-hand column. You can write as much or as little as you'd like. I'll give you just a few minutes for this. Then, when I give a signal, move to the right-hand column. Brain storm all the good things about the person.

Give the students the handout that follows (printable handout available at https://www.routledge.com/9781138305083). Give the students time, with more time for the positives than for the negatives. If they struggle to find things they like, make some suggestions – even small things (e.g., my teacher ends class on time). At the end, encourage students to keep searching for the good things about that person, keeping in mind that the person is not all bad.

Good vibes

Think about a person that you really dislike – they get under your skin, and they make life miserable for you. Take a few minutes and brain storm all the things you dislike about the person in the left-hand column (e.g., "my teacher talks too fast"). You can write as much or as little as you'd like (use the back of the page if needed). Then, in the right-hand column, think about the things you like (e.g., "my teacher is very passionate").

Things I hate	Things I like

Activity 4: Band-aid solutions

Purpose: To understand the difference between equality and equity and help students understand that other students might receive different treatment at times to meet their needs.

Materials: *Equality vs. equity* image (below and printable handout available at https://www.routledge.com/9781138305083); a box of band-aids.

Suggested time for completion: 10–15 minutes.

Introduction

One complaint that students often have is that a teacher treats them unfairly. We have a strong sense of justice and fairness, which begins very early in life (think of a young child complaining over his sister getting a bigger biscuit than him) and carries on throughout life. When we are treated fairly, we feel a sense of respect. A lack of fairness can drive feelings of jealousy, bitterness, and division.

At times, individuals and groups certainly are treated unfairly. Teachers need to be aware of ways they might be favouring one student over another, taking sides, or otherwise being unfair. But at other times, students have the *perception* that things are unfair. Often, we don't see the full picture. For instance, Alicia is allowed to turn in assignments late, but Sally gets penalised when she submits an assignment two days late. She complains that Mr Franco is so unfair. But Mr Franco knows that Alicia has a learning disability and needs extra time to get through things, and has set up an alternative submission schedule. Students come to school with a diverse set of needs and treating them all the same can be unfair.

This is the difference between *equality* (all are treated equally, regardless of needs and backgrounds) and *equity* (adjustments are made for different needs and backgrounds). This activity teaches students the difference between equality and equity, helping to develop understanding of why a teacher might seemingly treat them unfairly compared to another student (Activity adapted from Niaura, n.d. Image from Robert Wood Johnson Foundation, 2017).

Instructions

Begin by asking a few students to share about a time they felt they were treated unfairly. What happened? How did they feel? Acknowledge their experiences, especially any stories where the student indeed was treated in an unfair way.

Note that we like to be treated fairly, and when others get special treatment, it can make us feel bad. We wonder why that person is special, and it makes us feel bad about ourselves. But sometimes, we don't see the full picture. We might think things are unfair, but it's because we don't know the whole story.

Ask students to imagine that we have several different people – one is in a wheelchair, one is a big man, another is a petite woman, and a fourth is a child.

We want to be fair, so we treat them all *equally* by giving them each a push bike. What would happen? [ask for responses]

Show the *Equality vs Equity* image (below; printable version available at https://www.routledge.com/9781138305083). Explain that we each have different needs, and it's actually unfair if we are all treated the same way. *Equity* means that we each have the same outcomes (being able to ride the bike), but how we reach that outcome is adjusted to our unique needs. This is the difference between *equality* and *equity*.

Next, demonstrate this more directly. Invite students to pretend that they accidentally cut themselves. Go to the first student and ask where they are injured. Place a band-aid over the imagined wound. Go to the second student and ask where they are injured. Then, place a band-aid over the *same place* as the first student, regardless of where the second student says they are injured. Repeat for multiple students, always placing the band-aid in the same spot as the first student, rather than where the student indicates is injured.

Bring the students back together and ask if the band-aid actually helped them. Note that you helped all of them the same. Students should indicate that they were injured somewhere else – putting a band aid over your finger when your leg is cut doesn't do anything.

Finally, explain that there are times when you or other teachers give different students different things during the year because they have different needs, just like you needed a band-aid in a different spot.

Equality versus equity

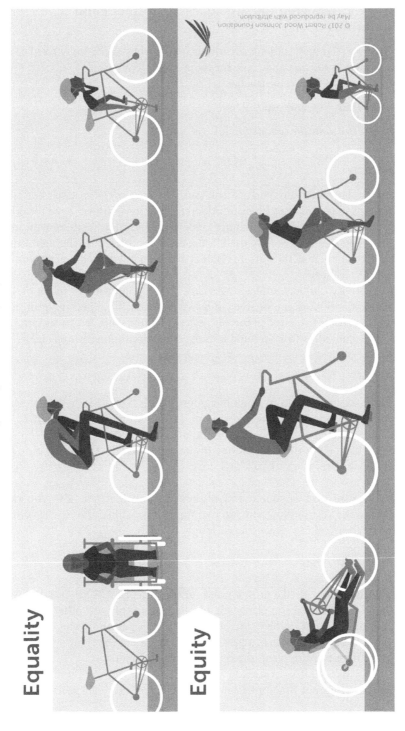

Equality

Equity

Figure 1.3 Examples demonstrating the difference between equality and equity

Activity 5: Drawing on past successes to fuel good relationships

Purpose: To help students identify ways that they successfully fixed a relationship in the past and apply the same strengths and skills to improve their relationship with their teacher.

Materials: Pen and paper.

Suggested time for completion: 20–30 minutes.

Introduction

It's easy to let friendships and acquaintances go over trivial matters, but when we want to maintain friendships or important relationships, we need to address issues in a positive, proactive manner. This exercise aims to help students identify skills that they successfully used in the past to repair a challenging relationship and to apply it to the current context and help build stronger relationships with their teachers.

The activity can be completed working one-on-one with a student or with pairs of students working together. It uses a peer coaching (peer-to-peer mentoring) approach to consider past successes, identify what led to success, and apply the same ideas to help build a stronger relationship with a teacher.

Instructions

Begin by asking students to think of a good friend. Next, ask them to describe what they do to maintain their friendship. For instance, perhaps they hang out together and keep each other up-to-date on social media.

Next, have them think about one of the times that the friendship didn't go so well. Ask them to think of a time that:

> You were mad at your friend or they were mad at you. But you cared about the relationship and patched things up. Think about what you or your friend did to make things right.

Share the following:

> Relationships are like growing and caring for a plant. Without water, sunlight, and nutrients, a plant will die. Relationships with other people are the same way. It involves listening to the other person, talking with them, and caring about them as a person. If you don't put effort into the relationship, then like the plant, the relationship will suffer.
>
> Just like with your friends, when things don't go well with a teacher, you need to put in effort. Fortunately, you can use your past successes to help you.

Next, help students to think about a time in the past when they successfully fixed a relationship, using the following questions:

- Think about a time when you needed to repair a relationship. Perhaps it was with a parent, a friend, or a teacher. How did you feel at the time the relationship was broken?
- How did it affect your life? School work? Home life? Other friendships?
- What did you do to fix things?
- What strengths did you use to fix things?
- What things can you do to strengthen your relationship with your teacher? Can the things you used in the past help in the current situation?

Help students brainstorm a list of possible ideas on ways to strengthen their relationship with a teacher. Guide the discussion to recognise what actions were successful in the past, and challenge them to consider how similar actions could be used with their teacher. Examples might include writing the teacher an email, asking to see the teacher after class for help, following instructions asked by the teacher, listening to the teacher, asking questions in class, smiling at the teacher, greeting him or her in the morning.

Once a list has been established, have them pair up with another student. One will be the coach. Invite them to guide the other student through the questions. Switch roles.

Bring students back together and invite them to trial one or two ideas over the next week, then follow up with their partner at a subsequent time.

If working with an individual student, work through the questions, brainstorming ideas together, and then asking the student to choose one or two things to trial over the next week and follow-up how they went in a future session together.

Activity 6: The life of a teacher

Purpose: To help students develop empathy for their teachers.

Materials: None.

Suggested time for completion: 30–40 minutes.

Introduction

One of the challenges to student–teacher relationships is that students often have unrealistic expectations of the teacher. This activity is designed to place the student in the shoes of the teacher. The activity aims to build empathy by helping students to recognise that teachers are human beings and have flaws and a life beyond the school's gates. The activity involves listening to a story, then talking through a set of questions. The story shows that the teacher struggles and engages in normal human activities just like everyone else. They may even have some mornings where they would prefer to stay in bed!

Instructions

Read the following passage about Sally without revealing the purpose of the activity, and then discuss the questions below.

About Sally

Sally wakes up at 6.30 a.m. She looks at her iPhone briefly and quickly scans Facebook to see what her friends and family are up to. It's still dark outside. Checking the temperature gauge, it's only 5 degrees. It's pouring rain. Her throat aches, and she wonders if she's getting a head cold. She wants to stay in bed and have a relaxing day at home. She imagines a day sitting in front of the heater, sipping hot cocoa, and reading a good book.

But a sense of responsibility propels her to the shower. She tries to motivate herself with music, and manages to get dressed and neatly groomed, but still feels exhausted and weary-eyed. She regrets staying up too late last night.

She forces down a smoothie, knowing she needs the energy for the day. She hops in the car, fights the traffic. A car honks at her, another car cuts her off, and she is delayed by the train. With growing frustration, she arrives at her destination at 7.30 a.m. It is still bitterly cold, and the sun has only just begun to rise.

She greets other colleagues and settles into her classroom, planning lessons, preparing the room, tidying up the constant mess of her students. She'll push through a long day, leaving work after the sun has set, spend time marking papers, before collapsing into bed. She is a teacher.

At 8.45 a.m., the students fill her classroom with chatter. Some are ready to go, others drag in, unprepared and grumpy about being there. The moods don't faze her. She's filled with a sense of purpose, driven to help her students learn. Her desire to stay in bed fades. She is much more excited about starting the school day once her students have arrived.

Discussion questions

- Were you surprised to find out that Sally was a teacher?
- Who did you think she was when the story began?
- Is starting the school day easy or hard for Sally?
- What do you think she would rather do in the morning?
- Why do you think Sally became a teacher?
- What challenges do teachers face at home?
- What challenges do teachers face at school?
- Do you think empathy (walking in someone else's shoes) helps with your appreciation and understanding of teachers?

Activity 7: Radio show host

Purpose: To help students get to know more about their teachers.

Materials: Pen and paper.

Suggested time for completion: 30–40 minutes.

Introduction

Students often know very little about the lives of their teachers and some self-disclosure (within professional limits) can enhance the student–teacher relationship. In this activity, students pretend to be a radio host and ask questions to a teacher to find out more information about them. This activity can be a fun one to run with you as the interviewee, or by bringing in another teacher or counsellor. At its core, this activity aims to allow students to see teachers as "real people".

Instructions

Ask your student to imagine that they were a radio show host, doing a "get to know you" segment on their show. The goal is to interview one of their other teachers. Ask students to choose a teacher they do not know a lot about. If you are working with an individual, ask them what questions they would want to ask a teacher? What would they want to find out? Give them time to come up with a list of questions, giving some suggestions as needed.

If you are working with a group, it can be fun if they interview you, or alternatively bring in a colleague. Give students time brainstorming ideas and come together to share their responses with one another, coming up with a final set of questions.

If you are the interviewee, have fun with this. Let students ask questions, be a bit vulnerable, and show that you are a real person. This can be scary to do, but helps give students a sense of you as a real person.

For other teachers, if possible, bring that teacher in and let the students interview the teacher, using the questions they came up with. If others are not available, encourage the students to follow up over the next week and interview their teacher with the list of questions, reporting back on their findings the next week.

Activity 8: About me

Purpose: To get to know more about each student.

Materials: Pen and paper.

Suggested time for completion: 20–30 minutes.

Introduction

Strong student–teacher relationships involve teachers who understand and know their students. As part of this, teachers need to know their students as individual people – what they like, what they dislike, who they are as a person. It's hard to support students that you don't know – you guess, but it's helpful to know first-hand, from their perspective. This exercise helps students proactively show their teachers who they are, by telling a bit more about themselves, by writing a letter about themselves.

Instructions

Ask your students to write a letter to a teacher who they would like to build a stronger relationship with. Guide students to let them know who they are, what they like, what they don't like and what they would like to achieve from their class. Students should mention also what they like best about the teacher they are writing to.

Module wrap up: Suggested questions for personal reflection or discussion

1   How do the activities change the way you feel about teachers?
2   What is one skill that you think you could take away and apply to your relationship with your teacher?
3   Do you think that teachers have the sole responsibility of building positive relationships with their student? Why/Why not?

Final thoughts

It is important to understand that the student–teacher relationship can also be effectively increased when teachers have a role to play. The exercises in this chapter provide students with ways to build positive relationships with their teachers, but the onus is not only on the students. Teachers need to have time for these activities, and it needs to be clear in the school environment that student–teacher relationships are valued. Don't underestimate "getting to know you" or "warm and fuzzy" types of activities. Bonding is important and can be an important conjugate to authentic and productive learning opportunities.

We would be remiss not to mention that there are times when teachers do not like their students. We would be unrealistic to suggest that every teacher enjoyed the company of every student, especially those that deviate from typical behaviour. Teachers are human beings and stress, ongoing challenging behaviour, and an unsupportive work environment can contribute to a negative outlook toward particular students. We ask that if you are a teacher or know of a teacher that feels this way towards a student that they seek further help. Does the student need to be connected to the learning support coordinator for support? Does the teacher need to seek advice from a supervisor, peer or mentor? Is the teacher's own personal wellbeing and self-care in check? Is the teacher mitigating external stressors that may be impact their relationship with a student or students? Does the teacher need external help? If a teacher is reporting toxic feelings towards a student, there may be me more going on and additional support may be needed.

References

Allen, K. & Kern, M. L. (2017). *School belonging in adolescents: Theory, research, and practice.* Singapore: Springer Social Sciences.

Allen, K. A., Kern, P., Vella-Brodrick, D., Waters, L., & Hattie, J. (2018). What schools need to know about belonging: A meta-analysis. *Educational Psychology Review, 30*(1), 1–34. doi: 10.1007/s10648-016-9389-8

Cemalcilar, Z. (2010). Schools as socialization contexts: Understanding the impact of school climate factors on students' sense of school belonging. *Applied Psychology: An International Review, 59*(2), 243–272.

Crouch, R., Keys, C. B., & McMahon, S. D. (2014). Student–teacher relationships matter for school inclusion: School belonging, disability, and school transitions. *Journal of Prevention & Intervention in the Community, 42*(1), 20–30. doi: 10.1080/10852352.2014.855054

Hattie, J. (2009). *Visible learning: A synthesis of meta-analyses relating to achievement.* London: Routledge.

Niaura, D. (n.d.). Teacher uses band-aids to explain difference between equality vs equity, 8-year-olds understand it better than adults [weblog]. *Bored Panda.* Retrieved from https://www.boredpanda.com/equality-equity-band-aid-student-lesson

Robert Wood Johnson Foundation. (2017). *Visualizing health equity: One size does not fit all infographic.* Retrieved from https://www.rwjf.org/en/library/infographics/visualizing-health-equity.html#/download

2 Connecting with parents

My dad was extremely enthusiastic about school and his approach to his own learning. I think that helped motivate me to succeed at school.

~ Shae, age 18

Module at a glance

In brief

This module explores parent-child relationships and suggests ways to foster positive emotions and build or strengthen their connection.

Learning outcomes

- Assess connectedness with parents.
- Identify ways to develop better connection.
- Recognise and use own strengths to enhance parent-child relationship.

Contents

A case study: Julia and her mum

Julia was a 15-year-old girl at an urban independent school. At least one morning most weeks, she would burst into the school psychologist's office in distress. Hot tears streamed down her face as she recounted an argument she had just had with her mother on their long drive into school.

Inevitably, Mum would soon follow. Equally distressed, but grateful that Julia was reaching out to someone else. Tears would stream down their faces, both devastated by the conflict. After spending a few minutes diffusing emotion, they would make up, embrace each other, and their relationship was restored for another day.

Conflicts between parents and their adolescent children are fairly usual. The "fights", as Julia called them, were mostly about her struggling with parental boundaries being laid. She wanted to spend more time with her boyfriend and her mum wanted her to spend more time on her schoolwork. But less conventional was the dramatic way in which grievances would play out. Yes, conflict erupted, but the response – both being devastated and working quickly to restore the relationship – was less typical. Why? Underpinning their relationship was a deep enduring bond. There was fear on both sides that the one person they loved possibly more than any other in the world was upset with them.

What the research says

Long-term relationships are not dependent on the amount of conflict that occurs. Conflict is a normal part of most relationships, as two individuals navigate understanding and appreciating the other person's perspective, needs, and way of being. What matters for the relationship is how conflicts are managed. Healthy parent–child relationships include open communication, feeling cared for, and a greater proportion of positive than negative interactions.

In our meta-analysis (Allen, Kern, Vella-Brodrick, Hattie, & Waters, 2018), we found that parent support was indeed an important factor underpinning a sense of school belonging. Studies suggest that students feel more connected to their school when there are positive communication channels open between the school and parents. Our research also found that parents who demonstrated care, were supportive, valued education, and encouraged school-related endeavours created a stronger sense of school belonging in their children.

Interestingly enough, we found that parent support actually had a stronger impact on school belonging than peer support. As adolescents increasingly develop independence and a sense of identity, parents play a less central role. But part of what makes the transition from childhood to adulthood successful is the support from parents, caregivers, or other close adults.

For example, highlighting the importance of the parental relationship, a four-year study followed two Australian Indigenous boys from childhood to early adolescence (Bell-Booth, Staton, & Thorpe, 2014). Both boys were from socially marginalised communities and were considered at high risk for educational disengagement, but had contrasting school experiences due to varying levels of parenting support. One boy had a very supportive family, who cared for the boy and did whatever they could to help support him through school despite limited educational experiences from both parents, displacement from home land, and transient living arrangements that resulted in frequent homelessness. The other came from an unstable home, an environment characterised by domestic violence, alcohol misuse, and unemployment with little parental support for his schooling. You can guess which one felt more connected to school and experienced greater academic success.

Stanković-Đorđević (2013) conducted a study with students with developmental disabilities. Perhaps not surprisingly, the mothers of children with disabilities were more likely to suffer from anxiety than mothers of typically developing children. The level of anxiety related to the child's sense of school belonging – the more anxious the mother was, the less connected to the school the child felt. With anxious or otherwise at-risk parents, schools may have to make special efforts to help both the child and the parent to feel comfortable with and connected to the school. It's not just the child's mental health that can create disconnection – parents' mental health also matters.

In sum, a student's relationship with his or her teachers, parents, and fellow students has been found to be meaningfully and positively related to school belonging. Parents play a key role in making the young person feel safe, cared for, and accepted as the adolescent swims through the choppy waters of secondary school.

Module overview

Adolescents often report that their parents "let them down", "worry too much", or "or stress them out". Sometimes parents carry their own anxieties, quirks, attributes or differences that make them . . .well, normal. While parent–adolescent conflict arises in part from a divergence between each person's individual needs, some of the conflict may also emerge from the young person's unrealistic perceptions and expectations about their parent.

This module aims to help young people recognise how important their parents/ caregivers are for supporting them, understand that parents and caregivers are human beings – imperfect, with numerous flaws and failings – and actively take steps to maintain a positive relationship. Throughout the module, we use the word "parent", but this may refer to one or more parents, step-parents, grandparents, caregivers, and so forth.

The module begins with an activity that helps create positive emotion and connection, and then provides a brief measure for the student to consider their relationship with their parent. The subsequent activities focus on recognising the strengths in their parents and developing skills to actively pursue positive relationships with them. They can be used with individuals or with groups.

Activity 1: Hot potato memories

Purpose: To bring up fun memories with parents and foster positive emotions.

Materials: Small bean bag or soft ball, music player.

Suggested time for completion: 20–30 minutes.

Introduction

Some students have a positive or negative relationship with their parents, while other students report a more tumultuous relationship that can shift and change rapidly depending on the hour or the day. Adolescents are forming their identity, and often at least give an impression of being independent from their parents to their peers. Rather than focusing on current relationships, this icebreaker activity takes a stroll down memory lane, bringing up fun memories and reminding students about the characteristics that they value in their parents. The activity brings in movement, fostering positive emotion and cooperation.

Instructions

Have the students form a circle. Ask them to think of a positive memory that they have about their parent. It can be recent or from a long time ago. It should be something that makes them smile – a fond memory. After giving students a moment to think, it's time for the game to begin. Play the music and ask a student to pass or gently toss the bean bag to another student. This continues until the music stops (stop it occasionally – vary which student it stops at). Whoever is holding the bean bag when it stops must share their memory. After a student shares, have everyone clap to celebrate the memory, and then start the music and pass the bean bag again.

If the bag falls on a student who already shared, have them toss it to someone else in the circle. Most likely, not all students will have time to share, but try to allow as many to share as possible. However, be sensitive to students who are clearly uncomfortable. Some students with poor or non-existent parental relationships might not have good memories. Allow them to pass or encourage them to share a positive memory of another adult in their life.

Activity 2: The parent connectedness scale

Purpose: To help students consider how well they connect with their parents.

Materials: *Parent connectedness scale* (below, printable handouts available at https://www.routledge.com/9781138305083).

Suggested time for completion: 20–30 minutes.

Introduction

Adolescence is a time when relationships with parents start to shift. Relational quality can range from excellent to non-existent – or depend on the day, hour, location, and circumstance. This activity provides a quick check on how connected the student feels with their parent. It gives students a way to stop and consider the positive qualities of their parents, and can help give you a sense of which students have good relationships and which ones are struggling. For students who recognise that their parents care about them and there is little conflict, then subsequent work should focus on developing skills to maintain and deepen connections with their parents. For students with poor relationships, you might focus more on helping students repair and develop a better relationship (when possible), or accept what is beyond their control and find alternative people to connect with.

Instructions

The *Parent connectedness scale* is provided below. Administer the survey at the beginning of the module, and then again at the end to consider how responses have changed over time. (Printable handouts available at https://www.routledge.com/9781138305083.)

Introduce the scale using the following script:

> How is your relationship with your parents or primary caregiver? Please read each statement carefully and then rate how strongly you agree or disagree. There are no right or wrong answers, but it will be most useful if you are honest.

The parent connectedness scale

This scale asks you to consider your relationship with your parents and caregivers. Focus on the primary person or people that you live with – whoever you consider to be your primary caretaker. Rate how much you agree or disagree with each of the following statements. Please be honest – there are no right or wrong answers!

1 I feel a strong sense of connection with my parent(s)/caregiver.

1	Strongly disagree	2	Disagree	3	Neither agree nor disagree	4	Agree	5	Strongly agree

2 My parent(s)/caregiver care about me as a person.

1	Strongly disagree	2	Disagree	3	Neither agree nor disagree	4	Agree	5	Strongly agree

3 I communicate well with my parent(s)/caregiver.

1	Strongly disagree	2	Disagree	3	Neither agree nor disagree	4	Agree	5	Strongly agree

4 I have a high-quality relationship with my parent(s)/caregiver.

1	Strongly disagree	2	Disagree	3	Neither agree nor disagree	4	Agree	5	Strongly agree

5 My parent(s)/caregiver support my learning.

1	Strongly disagree	2	Disagree	3	Neither agree nor disagree	4	Agree	5	Strongly agree

6 I feel close to my parent(s)/caregiver.

1	Strongly disagree	2	Disagree	3	Neither agree nor disagree	4	Agree	5	Strongly agree

7 I get along well with my parent(s)/caregiver

1	Strongly disagree	2	Disagree	3	Neither agree nor disagree	4	Agree	5	Strongly agree

8 I rarely have conflicts with my parent(s)/caregiver.

1	Strongly disagree	2	Disagree	3	Neither agree nor disagree	4	Agree	5	Strongly agree

Add up your scores to find your total: _____

Making sense of the results

After students complete the questions, have them add up their responses, scoring each as:

1 = strongly disagree

2 = disagree

3 = neither agree nor disagree

4 = agree

5 = strongly agree

General levels:

8 – 15 =	Low sense of connectedness
16 – 24 =	Moderate sense of connectedness
25 – 32 =	Fairly strong sense of connectedness
33 – 40 =	Very strong sense of connectedness

Have students reflect upon the following questions, either individually or in a group:

- Which questions did you agree with and which did you disagree with? What does this say about the quality of your relationship with your parents?
- Are you happy with your score, or are there areas that concern you?
- To what extent do you want to have a stronger relationship with you parents?

Activity 3: Getting to know me and you

Purpose: To help students understand and recognise their own character strengths and those of their parents.

Materials: VIA Youth survey and VIA Adult survey (www.viacharacter. org); *Strengths comparison* worksheet (below and printable handouts available at https://www.routledge.com/9781138305083).

Suggested time for completion: 30–60 minutes.

Introduction

Research in the field of positive psychology suggest that we have something called a "negativity bias". We are prone to look for the negative things that happen and the things that people do wrong. For example, imagine that you receive a set of student feedback on your performance as a teacher or practitioner. Most of the comments are extremely positive. But then one is very negative, providing scathing criticisms. Which comment do you focus on? Most likely the negative one.

We do the same thing with people. It's a lot easier to see the flaws in ourselves and others than their strengths. How often do we complain about our work, homes, friends and family, the weather, et cetera?

Yet the focus on the negative doesn't make us or others feel good. And this is where research from positive psychology can help us make a positive turn – by learning to recognise and value *strengths* within ourselves and others.

We are all good at different things. Maybe you are able to make people laugh. You enjoy being kind to others. You stick with things until they are done. You approach life with energy and zest. What is it that lights you up inside?

We all have strengths. To help identify what those may be, various lists of strengths have been developed. For example, the VIA Character Institute focuses on 24 strengths (see www.viacharacter.org). The website includes a survey to learn about your strengths, background information on each strength, the research behind the strengths, and lots of ideas on how to put the strengths into action.

Studies find that it can be valuable for both young people and adults to learn what their strengths are, use their strengths, and learn to recognise and value strengths in others. For the young person in the midst of developing their sense of identity, it's hard to have a positive sense of self when you are always being told everything you do wrong. It can be empowering for young people to know that there are good things about them.

A clear illustration of strengths in action can be found in the book *The Strengths Switch*. In the book, Professor Lea Waters at The University of Melbourne describes strength-based parenting – an approach to parenting that focuses on recognising and accentuating a child's strengths rather than their weaknesses. Drawing on personal experience and empirical research by herself and others, the book equips parents with strategies that focus on their child's strengths through various strategies. We certainly recommend the book for parents wanting to develop and maintain a positive relationship with their child.

But relationships go both ways. It's hard for Mum to feel valued when her daughter is more apt to notice that her mum is critical of her untidy room than to see the hard work she puts into ensuring the house is clean and orderly.

This activity is designed to help students recognise their own strengths and the strengths of their parents. It provides a foundation for developing a positive understanding and awareness of oneself and others. Activity 4 follows on from this, considering how strengths can be used to enhance students' relationships with Mum and Dad.

This is a lengthier activity, but one that is valuable to spend time on. It can also be useful to spend time discussing what the various strengths are. If needed, break this into two sessions, focusing first on one's own strengths, and then considering their parent's strengths at the second session.

Instructions

This activity makes use of the freely available VIA Character Strengths survey, available online at www.viacharacter.org. along with the *Strengths comparison* worksheet (see page 43; printable handouts available at https://www.routledge.com/9781138305083).

Have students go to the site and click on "Take the free VIA survey". This will bring up a registration page. Students will need to enter their name, email, and create a password, which will allow them to access their results in the future.

Instruct students to complete the registration information and then click on the Youth version of the survey (right hand option) and proceed through the questions. This takes about 15–20 minutes to complete. At the end, the student will receive a report noting an ordered list of their strengths. Have students write down their top five strengths on the *Strengths comparison* worksheet.

If you are working with a class or group of students, have the students pair up and share their top strengths with their partner. Ask the students to identify a time that they have used some of the strengths. Have one student tell a story about it to their partner. What happened, what did they do, and how did the strength help them? Then switch roles, allowing the other student to share their story.

If you are working with an individual student, have the student consider the top strengths. If needed, clarify what these mean (see the resources on the VIA website for details and ideas). Then, have them identify a time that they have used one of the strengths and tell a brief story about it. What happened, what did they do, and how did the strength help them?

Next, have students return to the main VIA webpage. Enter the same log-in information, and then click on taking the Adult version of the survey. Instruct students to choose one of their parents or caregivers and complete the questions *about that person*. This again will take 15–20 minutes to complete, and they'll receive a report with the ordered list of strengths. Again, have them write down their parent's top strengths on the strengths comparison worksheet.

Encourage students to spend a few minutes reflecting on the results. What are their strengths and those of their parent/ caregiver? Are they similar or different? What does this tell them about their parent/ caregiver?

If you are working with an individual student, have them tell a story about their parent that demonstrates a strength. If working with a group, have the students tell a story about their parent demonstrating one of the top strengths with their partner.

Encourage the student to look for strengths in their parents over the next week, noting examples down. Try to revisit this at the next session. Discuss what strengths they saw their parents exhibit, any of the ideas they tried out, and what the results of focusing on strengths were.

Strengths comparison worksheet

Complete the VIA Youth survey and discover your top strengths. Note them in the left column. Then complete the VIA Adult survey *about your parent/ caregiver*. Note their top strengths in the right column. Reflect on the results. Are your strengths similar or different to your parent? Anything you find surprising? What does it tell you about your parent/ caregiver?

My top strengths	My parent's top strengths
1.	1.
2.	2.
3.	3.
4.	4.
5.	5.

Reflections: _____

_____

_____

_____

_____

_____

Activity 4: Building strength-based relationships

Purpose: To help students identify strength-based approaches to enhance their relationship with their parent.

Materials: Completed *Strengths comparison* worksheet (see Activity 3), *Strength-Based Approach to my Parents* worksheet (printable handouts available at https://www.routledge.com/9781138305083).

Suggested time for completion: 20–30 minutes.

Introduction

Activity 3 helps students understand their own strengths and those in their parents. By recognising the strengths in oneself and others, it can help us focus on the positive sides of other people rather than on the things that annoy us.

But recognition is only the first part. Studies have found that there is considerable value in using one's strengths for the benefit of others. In this activity, we focus on using strengths to enhance the child–parent relationship, though the activity could be applied to other relationships as well (e.g., peers, friends, teachers).

Instructions

This activity builds on Activity 3. Have students reconsider their top strengths and the ones they identified in their parent/ caregiver. Review what the different strengths are (see the VIA website for detailed definitions and lots of resources on this).

Next, pick a few strengths (e.g., humour, appreciation of beauty, gratitude). Have students brainstorm ways they could use that strength to build a positive relationship with their parent. Then have students complete the *Strengths-Based Approach to My Parents* worksheet, coming up with ideas based on their top strengths or their parent's top strengths. It can be helpful for students to work with a peer or in small groups, sharing ideas and building upon each other.

Encourage students to try out one or more ideas with their parent over the next week. Revisit this at the next session, discussing what the results of a strengths-based approach were. Consider what worked and what didn't work. Note that a strengths-based approach takes practice. Encourage students to keep practising.

Examples of how the VIA character strengths can be used to enhance the parent–child relationship (see more ideas at www.viacharacter.org)

Strength	Examples of how to put it to use
Appreciation of beauty and excellence	Take a few minutes to think about what is beautiful or excellent in your parents. Think about what they have to offer that impacts on your life. Later today, tell them what you appreciate about them.

Bravery/ valour	After a disagreement, take the first step to initiate a resolution like saying sorry or expressing how you are feeling. Or ask your parent to talk and work together to create a change.
Creativity/ originality	Identify novel and fun ways that you can spend time together with your parent.
Curiosity/ openness to experience	Consider what your parent does that you are curious about. Ask them about it, and see if you can try it with them. Or consider something new that you and your parent might enjoy. Ask them to try it together with you.
Fairness	Think about the job that your parent has to do to be your parent. Think about a situation where you got mad at your parent. Were they being unfair, or was there a good reason for their action? What would be a fair way to respond? The next time you think you are being treated unfairly, take a deep breath and consider what a fair response would be.
Forgiveness	Consider the things your parent has done that you are angry about. Choose to let at least one of these go (This doesn't mean that they are right, but that you aren't going to hold on to it.)
Gratitude	Spend five minutes brainstorming what you appreciate about your parent. What are you grateful for? Later today, tell them one thing you appreciate about them.
Honesty/ integrity	Consider if there are ways you have lied or told half-truths to your parent. How can you share the truth?
Hope/ optimism	Try to say more hopeful and optimistic statements than negative and unhopeful statements in the course of the day. When you find yourself thinking about what might go wrong, shift your thought to think of what could go right.
Humility	Use your listening skills and try to do more listening than talking in a future conversation with your parents/caregivers. Does this give you any more insights into them? Admit your mistakes.
Humour/ playfulness	Humour and playfulness can be a great circuit breaker for conflict. It can be effective at lightening a moment. Try to incorporate this at an appropriate time.
Judgment/ critical thinking	Spend time thinking about what role you have to play in improving your relationship. Choose to take responsibility for what's within your control.
Kindness	Think about something that your parent would really enjoy – what would make them smile? Later today, engage in a kind act to pleasantly surprise them.
Leadership	Consider how you can take a leading role in admitting mistakes and how you can actively work to improve your relationship with your parent.
Love	Express love to your parent, either in a note or verbally.
Love of learning	Think about relationships as being something that takes time and work to improve. What relationships skills could be learnt to help improve your relationship?

(continued)

(continued)

Strength	Examples of how to put it to use
Perseverance	Keep working to improve your relationship. Try one strategy, and if that doesn't work, keep trying others. Stick with it despite challenges along the way.
Perspective/ wisdom	Put yourself in your parent's shoes. How would your parent/ caregiver feel about the situation? What kind of relationship would they like to have?
Prudence	During conflict, make a conscientious effort to think before you speak. If provoked, count to ten before responding, taking several deep breaths.
Self- regulation/ self-control	When you feel yourself becoming upset, regulate your reaction. Take several deep breaths – count to seven as you breathe in, hold your breath for four counts, then count to eight as you breathe out. Repeat this several times.
Social intelligence	Be aware and able to acknowledge that your parent is only human and has feelings too. Tune into what they might be struggling with or what they might be thinking or feeling, and how that might be impacting their behaviour.
Spirituality/ purpose	Go for a walk in the park or bush with your parent and discuss how being in nature makes you feel.
Teamwork/ citizenship	Imagine that you and your parents/caregivers are a team and need to work together in order to both be happy. Chat with your parent about ways to work together.
Zest/ enthusiasm	Be willing to do an activity with your parent and show energy and enthusiasm toward the activity.

A strength-based approach to my parents worksheet

How can you use your top strengths to build a positive relationship with your parent? Jot down as many ideas as you can think of. Then put a star next to one or two that you will try out over this next week.

My strengths	Ways to use the strength to build positive relationships

Activity 5: Fun times together

Purpose: To identify activities students enjoy doing with their parents.

Materials: Journal or personal notebook.

Suggested time for completion: 20–30 minutes.

Introduction

There are some parents who have good intentions but are unsure about how to really connect with their adolescent child. They want to be involved, but fear being overly involved. They want to do activities together, but fear that the activities they suggest are perceived as boring. Or they make their child do activities that are boring, creating a deeper sense of division and animosity. To help bridge gaps between a parent's good intentions and a student's interests, this activity involves asking the student to generate activities that they enjoy and would be willing to do with their parent. It asks the young person to consider what they have in common with their parent.

Instructions

Have students complete this activity in a journal or personal notebook. Introduce the activity using the following script:

> Being a parent is hard work. You want to connect with your children and be a part of their lives, but don't always know the best way to do that. Some parents back off, trying to not get in the way, others try too hard. Think about your parents. What are their interests? What are things you have enjoyed doing with them in the past, or really wish they would do with you now? Are there activities that you both enjoy, that you could consider doing together? For example, going out for pizza, seeing a movie, taking a class together, doing a jigsaw, or having a cuppa. Take a few minutes to think about activities you might enjoy doing with your parents, and then make a list in your journal or notebook.

After a list has been created, challenge students to find a time to sit down with their parent to discuss the list. Invite them to have a conversation with their parent, highlighting their own interests, the interests they see that their parents have, and how some of those overlaps can help build a strong, positive relationship.

Activity 6: Underlying messages

Purpose: To help students understand good intentions that might underlie their parents' actions.

Materials: None.

Suggested time for completion: 20–30 minutes.

Introduction

Most parents have good intentions, however the decisions they make may not always be positively received by their children. This mismatch in thinking can lead to conflict. This activity uses a hypothetical situation to help students think about the good intentions that might underlie a parent's seemingly unfair actions.

Instructions

First, read the following scenario:

> Joanie is 15. Although she goes to bed at 9.30 p.m. on school nights, she often stays awake until 2 a.m., as she texts her friends, stays up-to-date on the latest news and gossip through Snapchat and several other social media platforms, and occasionally plays games. But this means she's missing out on sleep. At school, Joanie is finding it hard to concentrate because she feels sleepy. She complains to her mum that she is tired.
>
> Her mum is concerned. She notices dark circles around Joanie's eyes and the fact that she has been yawning during the day. She's also aware of Joanie's phone use at night time. Wanting to help, she creates a plan to keep Joanie's phone out of the bedroom. At 9.30 p.m., Joanie's mum will plan to take Joanie's phone and keep it in another room overnight. That way, Joanie won't be distracted and will be able to get the sleep she needs.
>
> But as she raises the plan, Joanie is furious. She thinks it is unfair that her mother will take *her* phone, believing her mum has no right to do such a thing. She begs to keep her phone, believing her mum is uncaring and mean.

Next, discuss the following questions:

1   What are your thoughts about this situation?
2   Why has Joanie's mother removed the phone?
3   How do you think Joanie feels?
4   If you experienced a similar situation, would you feel the same as Joanie? Why/why not?
5   What are Joanie's mother's intentions (e.g., was she protecting Joanie, looking after her health, wanting to punish her)? Does Joanie understand these intentions?
6   How could this situation be resolved in a way that both Joanie and her mother can be satisfied?

Next, encourage students to spend a few minutes in personal reflection.

> Think of conflict you have had with your parent or care giver. What might have been the intentions of your parent or caregiver? Did they have your best interests in mind, even if you didn't agree with them?

Finally, end with a final take home message:

> Seeing things from other people's perspectives allows you to think about the intentions of other people. Often these intentions are coming from a good place. By stopping and taking time to understand their intentions it can help us not to feel so angry and automatically assume that things are unfair.

Activity 7: Unhelpful thoughts cheat sheet

Purpose: To recognise irrational and unhelpful thoughts and formulate alternative thoughts.

Materials: The *Unhelpful thoughts cheat sheet* worksheet (which follows, and printable handouts available at https://www.routledge.com/97811 38305083).

Suggested time for completion: 20–30 minutes.

Introduction

A lot of anger and frustration with parents can come from ruminating on thoughts that are irrational, inaccurate, and not particularly useful. When shared with outsiders, such thoughts can usually be identified as irrational or rational, but when we are caught up in our own thoughts, we can persuade ourselves they are true. This activity aims to help students to recognise some of their irrational and inaccurate thoughts, and to challenge them to think of alternative possibilities.

Instructions

Invite students to share some of the negative thoughts they have had about their parents (e.g., my parents don't want me to have fun). Let one or two students share, then ask if others have ever had the same thought. Next, have students brainstorm alternatives (e.g., my parents want me to do well in school. They want to make sure I get enough sleep at night). Go through several examples.

Next, provide students with the worksheet that follows (printable handouts available at https://www.routledge.com/9781138305083). Have them complete it individually or with a partner, identifying some of their negative thoughts and brainstorming one or more alternatives.

Finally encourage students to track their thoughts over the next week. Suggest to them that when negative thoughts come up, they should challenge them and think about alternatives, rather than just believing the first negative thought that arises.

The unhelpful thoughts cheat sheet

Do you ever find yourself frustrated with your parents? Perhaps you think it's unfair that they don't let you go out with your friends, or that your siblings always get away with everything, or you can't stand it when they insist on giving you a kiss before driving off. The thoughts turn over inside your head, making you angrier and angrier at your parents.

While such thoughts might be based on something that is true, reflecting on it and allowing it to make you angry is not particularly useful. The trick is to start challenging unhelpful thoughts, shifting your focus to something that would be more useful.

On the left side of the table below, jot down negative thoughts that you have about your parents – the things that annoy and frustrate you. List out as many as you can think of.

Negative thoughts about my parents	Alternative thoughts

Now, reconsider one or more thoughts. Is there an alternative way of thinking about it? For instance, maybe you feel it's unfair that your parents won't let you go out with your friends in the evenings. Alternatively, maybe they know that you want to score well on an upcoming exam, but to be successful, you need to study. They know that if you go out with your friends, you won't complete your homework and you'll fail the exam. So they are placing boundaries there to help you.

When you find yourself angry with your parents, take a few minutes and consider whether there might be an alternative explanation or way of thinking about things that might be more useful for both of you.

Activity 8: Relay team

Purpose: To recognise the roles and responsibilities of each member of the family and identify ways to support one another.

Materials: Video player with Internet connection.

Suggested time for completion: 30–40 minutes.

Introduction

This activity uses an analogy of a relay race to consider the need for understanding one's role and responsibilities within the family, and how getting relationships right requires give and take by both parties.

Instructions

First, show the following video (3 minutes):

https://www.youtube.com/watch?v=DLr74l177oM

Next, read the following text:

That video shows various relay races. One team member runs their segment as hard as possible, doing their part for the team, then they pass the baton to their team member, who grabs the baton and takes off, running their segment and passing the baton on. Each team member has a role to play. As the runner approaches the transition, they check to see that the receiver is ready. They run a short distance together, and the giver firmly pushes the baton into their teammate's hand. The receiver has to be ready to run, taking off at just the right time, reach back and grasp the baton, and swiftly take off to run their segment. Both the receiver and giver must watch each other, perhaps exchanging a quick glance or a small nod to indicate they are ready. Both have duties to fulfil and these duties rely on each other.

When handled well, as occurred for several of the teams in the video, the baton gracefully passes from one to another. But as could be seen in the video, with an error on either part, the baton falls and the team is out of the race. Getting that transition right takes a lot of coordination and practice. A lot of time is spent understanding each other's running style and coming up with signals that can let the other person know they are ready.

Your family is like team members in that race. You, your parents, and your siblings each has their own duties to fulfil. Your parents might need to go to work, clean the house, or do the shopping. You might have responsibilities around the house, homework to complete, or have to care for your siblings. When someone is not pulling their weight, then the whole team (or family) falls down. And just like in the race, everybody has to give and take at different times. This means you need to understand your role and responsibilities in the family, when you need to give and when you need to take, and understand signals to coordinate and create a smooth relationship.

Have students discuss with a partner or reflect in their journals on the following questions:

1   How might your family be like a relay team?
2   What are your responsibilities in the family?
3   What are others in your family responsible for?
4   How can you support your family in their roles?
5   What sort of support do you need to fulfil your responsibilities?
6   How can you be more considerate of each other?

Module wrap up: Suggested questions for personal reflection or discussion

1   Parents are human and equally vulnerable to the same strengths and weakness as any other person. How has your feelings and thoughts towards your parents changed since completing this module?
2   What are some ways you could try to focus on your parents' strengths, rather than their weaknesses?
3   All relationships require time, effort and work. What are some things you can do to improve your relationship with your parent(s)?

Final thoughts

The activities in this module provide students with skills to better understand and appreciate their parent's perspective, helping students learn how to actively develop supportive relationships. Parents play an important part in a young person's life, and students benefit from recognising and valuing this form of support. Of course, some parents will not reciprocate or will misinterpret efforts by their child. These activities try to help young people take responsibility for their part in the relationship.

If you are working with a young person in an ongoing /short term basis we encourage you (with consent) to reach out to their parents. Share with the parent the important work you are doing, advise parents how they can also take a role in increasing the feelings of belonging towards school. Some ideas for parents to increase a sense of belonging in their children might include:

*   modelling a sincere love of education
*   showing an interest in what their child is learning
*   believing and expressing that their child is capable and can master their goals as capable individuals
*   being involved is school life where ever possible.

Relationships, of course, are a two-way street, and parents need to also do what they can to communicate well, listen to the needs of their children, and be caring and supportive. Some parents do this better than others and providing skills and resources for parents can be useful. But here we focus on helping students take control of what they can (e.g., their perceptions, behaviour patterns, and reactions to their parents), and accept the parts of their parents that they can't control. The activities may not be appropriate for every student. There can be a variety of other factors affecting the parent–child relationship, including physical or mental health considerations, mental disorders, personality issues, domestic violence, substance abuse, unemployment, inability to meet basic needs, or a variety of other concerns. Such factors often require intervention by trained professionals or relevant agencies.

References

Allen, K., Kern, P., Vella-Brodrick, D., & Hattie, J. & Waters, L., (2018). What schools need to know about belonging: A meta-analysis. *Educational Psychology Review, 30*(1), 1–34. doi: 10.1007/s10648-016-9389-8

Bell-Booth, R., Staton, S., & Thorpe, K. (2014). Getting there, being there, staying and belonging: A case study of two indigenous Australian children's transition to school. *Children & Society, 28*, 15–29. doi: 10.1111/j.1099-0860.2012.00441.x

Stanković-Đorđević, M. (2013). Anxiety of teachers and mothers as an indicator of the sense of school belonging in children of developmental disabilities. *TEME: Casopis za Društvene Nauke, 37*(2), 785–801.

3   Connecting with peers

My friends help me to belong to school because they will support me and help me and I will do the same for them.

Connor, age 13

Module at a glance

In brief

This module provides strategies to empower students to develop good peer relationships.

Learning outcomes

- Describe the unique strengths and positive attributes of others.
- Evaluate the role of students within the class or peer group.
- Demonstrate empathy, tolerance and understanding of other people.

Contents

A case study: The broken friendship

Another day in the school psychologist's office and another box of tissues quickly disappears. Molly sobbed as she reports that nobody likes her, she has no friends, and her friendship group always ignore her. Molly is in Year 8. This age group can be marked with the realisation that not everyone likes you and some peers or so-called friends can be "real jerks" (as Molly put it). Many students at this age are undergoing rapid maturation and still developing and learning social and emotional competencies that help build good friendships. As a result of this, friendships can come and go, and it is common for students to move between friends and social groups. When conflict does occur, it can be dramatic and deeply painful.

Molly and Jemima had known each other for over a decade. In fact, they first met as babies as their mums were in the same *mothers' group*. They started Prep together and then later attended the same local secondary school. Their mothers' friendship continued, and Molly and Jemima often saw each other outside of school.

But lately their deep friendship had fallen apart. This week, according to Molly, Jemima was giving her greasy looks and ignoring her. When asked if Molly had initiated any conversation or greetings (e.g., saying "hi" in the morning), Molly noted that she has been keeping her distance, not wanting to create more conflict and pain.

It seemed clear that Molly was feeling a sense of loss. Taking a problem-solving approach, the school psychologist helped Molly create a list of possible options that may help to patch things up. Strategies that were listed included: Molly talking to Jemima about their friendship, Molly texting Jemima or greeting her in the morning, and Molly writing a letter to Jemima to express the importance of their friendship. The pros and cons of each option was considered. As tears rolled down her face, Molly decided she'd rather meet Jemima in the school psychologist's office, with the school psychologist acting as a mediator. The psychologist agreed and contacted Jemima, who immediately agreed to the meeting.

Molly arrived for the meeting first and found a comfortable chair. Jemima arrived second. At first, each girl looked down, avoiding eye contact. But then one looked up and caught the eye of the other. They said coy "hellos", which soon turned to giggles and beaming smiles. By the end of the meeting, they walked out of the office linked arm-to-arm, not only reunited in their friendships, but also armed with strategies to prevent such conflict in the future.

What the girls really needed was a circuit breaker, and to some degree, the school psychologist fulfilled that role. Both felt the other was ignoring them and responded by withdrawing and ignoring the other. The meeting gave them a chance to recognise their own contribution to the problem, and to change the way they behaved towards each other in a way that was more authentic and genuine toward their feelings about their friendship. For instance, one strategy Molly and Jemima found useful was to remember to make eye contact and say hi to one another first thing in the morning. A simple acknowledgment, and yet very powerful for creating and maintaining connection with others.

What the research says

A search on school belonging through Google images brings up endless photos of smiling young people, arm-in-arm with their friends. The common view is that peers are the critical factor determining whether or not a student feels a sense of belonging at school. Interestingly, although peers do indeed contribute to a sense of belonging, our research indicates that support by teachers and parents made more of a difference than peers (Allen, Kern, Vella-Brodrick, Hattie, & Waters, 2018).

While at first this may seem counterintuitive, digging deeper, we see that it depends not only on having peers and friends, but also on the *type* of peers one associates with and the *quality* of relationships. For instance, a young person might be part of a peer group that does not value education, frequently skips class, and speaks disparagingly about teachers. In turn, the student feels increasingly disconnected from school, taking on the identity and perspective of their peers. Another young person might struggle to fit in with peer groups at school, but really enjoys the learning and receives considerable encouragement from his or her parents and teachers. They feel a sense of deep connection to the school, despite feeling disconnected from peers. The literature clearly shows that both friendships and peer relationships contribute to a sense of belonging (Brown & Evans, 2002; Libbey, 2004) – but this can be for better or worse, depending on what those relationships involve.

Peer pressure – which can be positive or negative – is a common part of adolescence. The right peer group can influence positive academic behaviours, which support learning and connection with the school, buffer the effect of negative peer pressure and facilitate young people to make positive decisions (Eccles & Gootman, 2002). Friendships thus can serve as an important protector against harm (Hamm & Faircloth, 2005).

But peers can also lead the young person astray, pulling the adolescent in adverse ways. In their work on school belonging, Roffey and Boyle (2018) made a distinction between inclusive and exclusive belonging. *Inclusive belonging* involves welcoming all people to a group, whereas *exclusive belonging* requires an individual to have particular attributes in order to join. At school, when adolescents are excluded from friendship groups, it can be a great source of stress.

We do see that it's important to have friends. Individuals who have several friends tend to be happier (Myers, 2000), have a greater sense of wellbeing (Diener, 2000), cope better with stress (Rubin et al., 1992) and report more favourable health and academic results (Vaquera & Kao, 2008) than those with no friends. Ueno (2005) found that friendships were associated with fewer signs of depression. Friendships not only play an important function in school belonging, but in the wellbeing of young people more generally. The key is to develop good peer relationships that create a sense of connection with others, motivation to learn, and desire to positively contribute to the world.

Module overview

Peers and friendships are an important part of the adolescent experience. Schools and teachers can play an important role in enabling positive peer relationships to develop. Supporting collaborative work, embedding friendship and relational skills in the curriculum, developing peer support and mentor programs, offering opportunities for inclusive clubs and groups, and equipping parents and teachers with strategies to navigate peer conflict when it arises, all contributes to the successful connection with peers.

This module aims to empower students with strategies to understand and value others and develop skills for relating well with peers. It emphasises the importance of supportive friendships, and helps students understand others' perspectives.

Activity 1: Rainbow ribbons

Purpose: To promote positivity and connection with others.

Materials: Ribbons (six colours, cut into various lengths, with a generous supply of each colour); index cards or sticky notes in six colours (match the paper colours to the ribbon colours).

Suggested time for completion: 30–60 minutes.

Introduction

Friendships can be transient, coming in and out of life, especially during adolescence. A friendship breakdown in Year 8 does not mean that the relationship will not remerge later, and best friends "forever" often do not last. Young people are learning who they are and how they fit with others – sometimes successfully, sometimes less so. Those who are perceived as different are at risk of exclusion and other forms of relational aggression (even if what is considered *normal* is constantly shifting).

Adolescents often desperately long to be accepted by others. To protect themselves, when signs of threat occur, they might react against and criticise others or alternatively withdraw from others. This activity encourages students to appreciate and acknowledge the unique strengths and positive attributes of others, building a sense of positivity and connection. This activity, originally adapted from the Butterfly Foundation's BodyThink program (https://thebutterflyfoundation.org.au/butterfly-resources/free-to-be-a-body-esteem-resource/) has been tried and tested many times over the last decade and each time has been a favourite by students and staff alike. The activity works best when students already know each other to some extent (i.e., an existing group or class, not as an initial get-to-know-you activity).

Instructions

Ask students to brainstorm characteristics they have noticed of a person who gets on really well with others – someone who is really likeable, perhaps a good friend. Write each one up on the board. If not mentioned, add several social characteristics:

- good listener
- considerate, thoughtful, caring
- helpful
- empathetic
- kind
- friendly.

Next, for each characteristic, check that the group agrees it's a desirable characteristic, excluding any of the silly ones. Ask students to agree on a colour that represents this characteristic (e.g., helpful might be orange, caring might be green). List one attribute for each card/ sticky note – you'll have several characteristics per each colour. Stick the notes on the wall or board.

Then, invite students to consider the attributes, and pick several they see in other students in the group. Have them take ribbons that match that attribute and tie the ribbon around somebody's wrist who matches that attribute. Students will need to tell the person why they have received a ribbon (e.g., "I think you are a calm person and that makes me feel comfortable around you"). Demonstrate this with a student, and then allow students to select ribbons and move around the room.

Encourage them to make sure nobody is left out and that they are giving ribbons to people who are not necessarily their friends. During the activity, keep an eye out for anyone not receiving ribbons – target those students with your own words of encouragement.

Bring the students back together and reflect on the activity. Ask a few students to share who they gave a ribbon to and why they gave the ribbon. Then ask:

1   How did you feel as the giver?
2   How did you feel as the receiver?
3   How can you apply this to the real world without ribbons?

Finally, give students a few minutes to reflect on the experience. Encourage them to wear their ribbons through the day as a reminder of the characteristics that others appreciate in them.

Activity 2: Being accepting and tolerant

Purpose: To develop empathy with others.

Materials: *Tolerance scenario cards* (printable cards available at https://www.routledge.com/9781138305083).

Suggested time for completion: 30–60 minutes.

Introduction

Schools are diverse places and students can come from a variety of backgrounds. Everybody has biases and prejudices that are often ingrained from a very early age and informed through culture and life experiences. Such biases may operate at subconscious levels – where we aren't directly aware of them, but they still impact how we respond to and interact with others. Unfortunately, this can lead to conflict, exclusion, and victimisation of students who are different.

One way to shift biases and prejudices is through raising awareness and exposure to others in a positive, constructive manner. This activity is designed to help students to become more mindful of their own biases; to consider equity, diversity, and tolerance; and to develop an awareness of and appreciation for the needs of others. The activity involves role play and reflection in pairs or small groups.

Instructions

Have students form groups of three to five. Hand out one *Tolerance scenario card* (below, printable version available at https://www.routledge.com/9781138305083) to each group (depending on the size of the group, there will be repeats). Invite the groups to read the scenario and consider several different responses.

Next, two students in the group should act out the scene on the card, providing one possible response. Change roles, acting out several different responses and several different outcomes. Encourage students to rotate through the roles, until all group members have played each role. Then the group should discuss the questions provided on the card.

Float between groups, adding suggestions or questions when students get stuck.

Bring the groups back together. Invite a few groups to act out their scene, providing a few alternatives. Discuss what other scenarios may occur at school, and possible responses/ outcomes.

Finally, ask the students to consider:

- How can you help everyone feel like they belong at school?
- What does an inclusive school look like?
- How can we show tolerance to those who might be different?
- How can we make sure we all show each other respect?

Tolerance scenario cards

Cindy and Maki

The scenario

An assessment task has been set for English class, and Mrs Grammar, the English teacher, has paired students up. Cindy is horrified to learn that she is to work with Maki, a new student from Japan. Maki speaks almost no English – she'll barely contribute. Cindy believes that her fate in this assessment is doomed. Whatever is she going to do?!

Role play

Select one person to play Cindy and one to play Maki. Act out an interaction between Cindy and Maki. Switch things up, so each of you play each role, acting out possible actions and responses, until each of you has played both roles.

Question discussion

After each person has played both roles, discuss the following questions:

- What might this situation be like for Cindy, and what might it be like for Maki?
- What is going to be difficult? How are they going to make the assignment work?
- What might help the girls to understand one another? How would this make Cindy feel? How would this make Maki feel?

Tom and Stephen

The scenario

Tom thinks Stephen is dumb. Stephen struggles to keep up in class, can never get his homework done, and his best mark in an assignment this term is a "C". The teacher takes Tom aside and explains that Stephen has a learning disability and struggles to comprehend words and numbers. The teacher asks Tom if he could sit next to Stephen and be his learning buddy.

Role play

Select one person to play Tom and one to play Stephen. Act out an interaction between Tom and Stephen. Switch things up, so each of you play each role, acting out possible actions and responses, until each of you has played both roles.

Question discussion

After each person has played both roles, discuss the following questions:

- What do you think school is like for Stephen? What would be difficult for him?
- What could Tom say to Stephen to help him?
- What might help the boys to understand one another? How would this make Tom feel? How would this make Stephen feel?

Tolerance scenario cards

Lisa and Ava

The scenario

Aya wears a Hijab and is a devout Muslim. She has lived in Australia her entire life and considers herself as Aussie as the other kids at her school. But other students tease her, calling her names, and making jokes about the foods she eats and her frequent visits to the Mosque. Lisa notices Ava's discomfort but doesn't know what to do to help.

Role play

Select one person to play Lisa and one to play Ava. Act out an interaction between Lisa and Ava. Switch things up, so each of you play each role, acting out possible actions and responses, until each of you has played both roles.

Question discussion

After each person has played both roles, discuss the following questions:

- What might Lisa ask to understand Ava's religion?
- What could Lisa say to students who are teasing Ava?
- How do you think Ava feels from the teasing? What might her life be like?
- What might help the girls to understand one another? How would this make Lisa feel? How would this make Ava feel?

Bonnie and Jodi

The scenario

Jodi has come to school late again and does not have the correct equipment. Bonnie heard a rumour that her father left the family with no explanation and has taken all the family's money. Bonnie notices that Jodi's school-dress is torn, and for lunch she only has some dry biscuits. After school, Bonnie sees Jodi waiting for her bus.

Role play

Select one person to play Bonnie and one to play Jodi. Act out an interaction between Bonnie and Jodi. Switch things up, so each of you play each role, acting out possible actions and responses, until each of you has played both roles.

Question discussion

After each person has played both roles, discuss the following questions:

- What do you think school is like for Jodi? What would be difficult for her?
- What could Bonnie say to Jodi to help her?
- What might help the girls to understand one another? How would this make Jodi feel? How would this make Bonnie feel?

Activity 3: Shifting perspectives

Purpose: To develop awareness, understanding and appreciation of others with different backgrounds, perspectives, and personalities.

Materials: *Blind men and the elephant* image; *Johari window* worksheet (below and printable worksheets available at https://www.routledge.com/9781138305083).

Suggested time for completion: 30–60 minutes.

Introduction

The way people perceive events and experiences can differ markedly from person to person. These perceptions are informed by past experiences, personal characteristics, and various other individual and social factors. A group of people may witness the same event, but each individual's interpretation of what has occurred may be different.

This activity first tells a story about different perspectives (*The blind men and the elephant*). The story suggests that we each can bring a different point of view to things. There can be truth to what someone else says, even if you don't think it's true. In the story, a group of blind men describe an elephant from what information they have access to. None of them have the whole truth – only by putting all their perspectives together do we gain a sense of what an elephant truly is – as an outsider would see it. When we disagree with others, we should accept that the other person may have a good reason for their beliefs and be open to their perspective. Perhaps your "truth" is wrong or is only part of the picture.

After considering the story, this activity then uses the Johari window, originally created by American Psychologists Joseph Luft and Harry Ingham. It is a popular tool in organisational settings, but we believe it has a lot of utility for students as well. The activity aims to highlight the unique perceptions that each individual has, helping to build empathy, tolerance and understanding towards the perspectives of others. It also provides opportunity for self-reflection.

Instructions

Begin with the story of the blind men and the elephant (Buddhist texts, date and origin unknown):

> Once upon a time, there lived six blind men in a village. One day the villagers told them, "Hey, there is an elephant in the village today."
>
> They had no idea what an elephant was. They decided, "even though we would not be able to see the elephant, let us go and feel it so we can find out what it is." The blind men went into the village to find the elephant so they could touch it.

"Hey, the elephant is a pillar," said the first man who touched his leg. "Oh, no! It is like a rope," said the second man who touched the tail. "Oh, no! It is like a thick branch of a tree," said the third man who touched the trunk. "It is like a big hand fan" said the fourth man who touched the ear of the elephant. "It is like a huge wall," said the fifth man who touched the belly of the elephant. "It is like a solid pipe," said the sixth man who touched the tusk of the elephant.

The blind men began to argue about the elephant and each man insisted that they were right. The men became agitated.

A wise man was passing by and saw the commotion. He stopped and asked them, "what is the matter?" The blind men said, "we cannot agree on what an elephant is." Each blind man took in turns to tell the wise man their perspective of what he thought the elephant was like. The wise man calmly explained to them, "you are all right. The reason you are describing the elephant differently is because you have all touched a different part of the elephant. So, actually the elephant has all the features you describe."

"Oh!" everyone said. The arguments stopped and the blind men felt happy that they were all right.

Lead students through a brief discussion of the blind men and the elephant story, with questions such as:

- The blind men argue over what an elephant is. Which one is correct? Why?
- What can we learn from the story?

End the discussion by emphasising that each person has unique perceptions of other people and events based on prior knowledge, learning and experiences. When we disagree with others, stop and consider that they may have a different perspective than you – there is value in discovering their perspective, rather than assuming they are wrong.

Next, introduce students to Johari's window: a technique developed by psychologists to help people see things from different perspectives. Explain the four quadrants:

- Quadrant 1 "Public": this refers to the characteristics, feelings, values and behaviours that you are aware of and others know about you.
- Quadrant 2 "Blind Area": this refers to characteristics, feelings, values and behaviours that others can see in you but you are unaware of.
- Quadrant 3 "Hidden Area": this refers to characteristics, feelings, values and behaviours that you know about yourself, but others do not know about you.
- Quadrant 4 "Unknown": this refers to characteristics, values, feelings and behaviours that you don't know about yourself, and others also do not know. We might make assumptions about ourselves and others, but really

don't know – we only discover these characteristics through our experiences and reactions in the future, yet they contribute to your perspectives and relationships with other people.

Next, form groups of two to four students (if working with an individual student, then you can be their partner). Distribute the *Johari window* worksheet (on page 69; printable handouts available at https://www.routledge.com/9781138305083). After they write their name on top, have them proceed through the following:

1   Individual reflection: Give 3–5 minutes for students to complete Quadrant 1 (Public) on their own. List 5 to 10 traits/values they believe are known to self and to others.
2   Peer feedback: Next, instruct everyone to pass their Johari Worksheet to the group member on their left. Give 1–3 minutes for that person to list one to two traits/values they see/observe/know about the owner of the paper in Quadrant 2 (blind areas), which they think the person might be unaware of. Then, students should pass the paper to the left, until everyone in the group has written on each other's worksheet. Use the back of the paper if needed.
3   Individual reflection: Give students 5 minutes to read the lists of others, then to complete Quadrant 3 (Hidden), listing traits or values known to themselves but unknown to others.
4   Leave Quadrant 4 (Unknown) blank. This is something for reflection, something they can think of about in the future.

Finally, discuss the following questions with students (or invite a few minutes of private reflection):

•   What did you think about the *Johari window*? Did you find the activity useful?
•   What did you learn?
•   How does the Johari window activity impact your thoughts and feelings of others?

The blind men and the elephant (visual image)

Johari window

Name: _____   **Date:** _____

PUBLIC	BLIND
HIDDEN	UNKNOWN

Activity 4: Human bingo

Purpose: To acknowledge the different strengths and personalities of one's peers.

Materials: *Human bingo* worksheet (below, printable handouts available at https://www.routledge.com/9781138305083).

Suggested time for completion: 25–40 minutes, or two sessions of 5 and 15 minutes, with student work in between.

Introduction

Peer groups can be diverse, with each individual bringing unique qualities to the friendship, class or group. This activity provides a fun way to encourage students to discover the unique attributes of their friends and peers, and helps them to consider the contributions that they and others bring to their own social world.

A classroom version of Human Bingo is described below. There can be several variants of the Human Bingo activity, depending on the time and resources available. Adding fun and creativity can make the activity more engaging. You might also consider:

- Making it a game by awarding small prizes to whoever fills it out first, the person with the most diverse set of responses, or other combinations.
- Introducing the activity in a group or class, and then assigning it as a homework task or an activity to complete during break times.
- Providing students with a digital copy. During the week, students can fill out the card, but rather than obtaining signatures, challenge them to take selfies with the person. Add the pictures to the digital copy then print out and bring to the group to share.

Instructions

Distribute the *Human bingo* worksheet (below; printable handouts available at https://www.routledge.com/9781138305083). Instruct students to think about people in class or group who could fit some of the descriptions described on the bingo card.

Then, give students 15–20 minutes to complete the card by obtaining the signatures of people who they think match the descriptions. When asking the person for their signature on a bingo square, the student should share why they selected them. Challenge students to find *different* people to complete each square.

Bring students back together. Discover who got Bingo (five squares in a row, horizontally, vertically, or diagonally), or even filled the full board. Ask a few students to expand upon a few of their answers. Encourage personal stories and anecdotes.

Finally, encourage some general reflection questions:

- How did you feel about this activity?
- What did you discover?
- How does this activity apply to real-life?

Someone who can be silly with me	A good listener	"The Joker" (tells weird jokes or just naturally funny)	The serious type	Most friendly
Likes to sing	My "foodie" buddy	The fashionista	My movie buddy	The most diligent in doing school work.
Someone who is very empathetic	Someone who always wear a smile.	★	Someone who is always positive	Someone who is loyal
Someone who can help others with maths	Someone who likes adventure	Someone who is my exact opposite	Someone who loves parties	Someone who likes to dress up
Someone who is kind	Someone who inspires me	Someone who's into sports	My childhood buddy	Someone who loves arts and crafts

Activity 5: Letters of appreciation

Purpose: To experience a reciprocal sense of satisfaction from appreciating others, showing gratitude, and noticing the positive presence other people bring to a group setting.

Materials: Pen and paper, scraps of paper, one bowl per table.

Suggested time for completion: 30–60 minutes.

Introduction

Think of the last time that you were pleasantly surprised when someone noticed and thanked you for something you had done. Perhaps it was something that you said or did, an act of kindness you showed towards another person. Maybe you worked hard, built or created something, or accomplished something meaningful, and someone else noticed and acknowledged what you did. Or maybe a student thanked you for the extra effort you put into the lesson. How did it make you feel to be acknowledged?

And think of a time when you thanked someone for something they did. How did you feel as you focused on what you appreciated and shared that with the person?

When someone shows gratitude or appreciation for something we have done, it often creates a sense of satisfaction for both the giver and the receiver. This activity helps students to experience the reciprocal benefits of appreciation and gratitude.

Instructions

Create groups of four to six students, grouping together students who may not ordinarily work together, but with whom they are familiar. Invite students to write their name on a scrap of paper, fold in half, and place in a bowl in the middle of the table. Then, each group member selects a name, returning the paper only if they select their own name.

Next, give students 10 minutes to write a short letter of appreciation to the person. Challenge students to describe what they appreciate about the person, focusing on their character, strengths, achievements, and behaviours, rather than appearance. They might recall a particular happy memory they share with the other student. They might express gratitude towards something the person has done for them. Make sure and include the name of the person the letter is about.

After 10 minutes, have students fold the letter in half and place in the middle of the table. Have one student shuffle the letters, and then each group member selects a letter to read (exchanging letters if they select their own name) and take turns reading the letters to the group.

Bring the groups back together. Invite a few students to share how they felt, both in writing the letter and in hearing their letter read out. Ask students to reflect on the lessons learned and how they can take this forward.

If you are working with an individual student, you can ask them to write a letter of appreciation or gratitude towards a friend of their choice. They should deliver their letter and reflect upon the experience at a later session.

Activity 6: Friendship reminiscing

Purpose: To help students positively process relational memories of the past, and connect with their peers through shared experiences and peer support.

Materials: *Friendship reminiscing* worksheet (printable handouts available at https://www.routledge.com/9781138305083), M&Ms (one pack per group).

Suggested time for completion: 30–40 minutes.

Introduction

We all have memories of different experiences with relationships. Some are inspiring and uplifting, others are sad or can even be traumatic, and some are bitter-sweet. Reminiscing on the past can help us make sense of our experiences and develop a narrative about who we are and what life means.

But reminiscing can be beneficial or harmful. Studies show that writing about memories – even very painful memories – can be beneficial. But when we ruminate on bad memories – thinking and rethinking about what happens– it can be harmful, both in how we feel and how we interact with others. In contrast, recounting memories, by putting them down on paper or sharing them with others, takes things out of our head. When we share a memory, it can connect us with others. You may discover that you have something in common with someone else or that you have had a similar experience. Discussing our memories can help us make sense of them and consolidate our thoughts and feelings. They can help us make decisions in the future.

This activity helps students to reflect on and make sense of some selected positive memories that they are willing to share about friendships. It also encourages students to connect and develop trust with each other.

Instructions

Introduce the activity by sharing a memory of one of your own friendships – either a positive or a challenging memory that resulted in a good outcome. Note that we all have memories of different experiences, both good and bad, but the focus on this activity is to look at the more positive memories students have had with friends as a way to build connections and look at how similar experiences can be harnessed in the future.

Distribute the *Friendship reminiscing* worksheet (on page 76, however a printable handout is available at https://www.routledge.com/9781138305083, which is recommended for the activity). Give students 10 to 15 minutes to work through the sections. Use the following instructions to guide students though the activity:

- In the first box, write down a positive memory about someone in the class or group.
- In the second box, write down a positive memory about one or more of your friends.
- In the third box, write down a funny memory with one or more friends – something that makes you laugh when you think about it.
- In the fourth box, write down challenging situations you shared with one or more friends that you were able to overcome and helped strengthen your friendship.
- In the fifth box, list down insights about the quality of your friendship(s) based on your memories and experiences.
- In the sixth box, write down your aspirations in building friendship with others that you will meet in the future.

Before you start this activity, pre-assign one task box to each M & M colour available. Give each group one pack of M & Ms. Instruct students to pass around the packet and pull out a colour. For the colour they pick, they will share to the group that particular experience or what they have written down in the corresponding box. For instance, if one member received a yellow M & M, he/she will share about a positive experience with a friend/friends. Then they can eat the M&M. Then it passes around the group until time is called. Give students 10–15 minutes to share. Note that they do not need to share anything they do not feel comfortable sharing – if uncomfortable, they can share one of their other responses.

Bring the students back together and reflect on the experience. What insights did they learn by reflecting on their experiences? What did they learn about their peers through the sharing? What was the most challenging aspect?

Friendship reminiscing

Fill out each of the following boxes, sharing one or more memories and thoughts.

1   A positive memory that you have with someone in your class/ group
2   A positive memory with one or more friends

3	A funny memory with one or more friends

4	A memory of a challenging situation with one or more friends that helped strengthen your friendship

5	Insights about the quality of your friendships

6 **Aspirations in building future friendships**

Activity 7: Categorical heuristics

Purpose: To help students understand ways we subconsciously categorise others, challenging them to explicitly think about who they include and who they exclude.

Materials: *Diverse people* image cards (printable handouts available at https://www.routledge.com/9781138305083 – print and cut out).

Suggested time for completion: 15–20 minutes.

Introduction

Walking or driving down the street, you might see people of all sorts of backgrounds. Sporty, studious, religious, rich, poor, foreign, married, single, young, old, hurried, lazy, distressed, oblivious . . . how do you categorise those that you see? Our environments are very complex, and our minds help us simplify the amount of information coming in through something called *heuristics* – mental shortcuts.

One such heuristic is how we categorise others. The categories we subconsciously create come from our own background and experiences. For instance, when you see a person wearing lycra and a helmet, you might assume that he is a cyclist. Perhaps you are an athlete and feel a sense of connection with a fellow athlete. Or perhaps cyclists annoy you – you think they inconsiderately take over the road, slowing down traffic and being in the way. You assume, therefore, that the person you see shares the same attributes or characteristics.

While heuristics help to conserve mental energy and save time, they can also get us into trouble, especially when we make judgments that are wrong. It can affect how we treat other people, in ways that are not always kind. We might exclude a person based on assumptions we make about them, without actually knowing anything about them. Teachers and students need to be careful about developing strong opinions about others without knowing them.

This activity helps students to identify ways that they may categorise others and consider how this might impact their interactions with others.

Introduction

Students might work individually, in pairs, or in small groups. You need one set of the *Diverse people* image cards for each group or student.

Invite students to sort through the photos and categorise them. Students should define the categories they create. Then, ask them to find another way to categorise them. Repeat several times. To add an element of competition, challenge them to come up with as many different ways to classify the pictures as possible, giving 5 minutes for the challenge.

Bring students together to discuss the activity. What categories did they come up with? Using one of the pictures, have students share the different ways that they categorised the picture. Explain that we are always categorising the people that we interact with. This is not a bad thing – it's a mental shortcut or *heuristic* – which helps conserve energy and save time.

But they can also get us into trouble, especially when we make judgments about others that are wrong. Discuss the possible implications of the different categories, and how it might lead to bad outcomes for you or that person.

End by emphasising the importance of recognising the categories we create and the impact that might have. Challenge students to take time to genuinely get to know people for who they really are.

Diverse people image cards

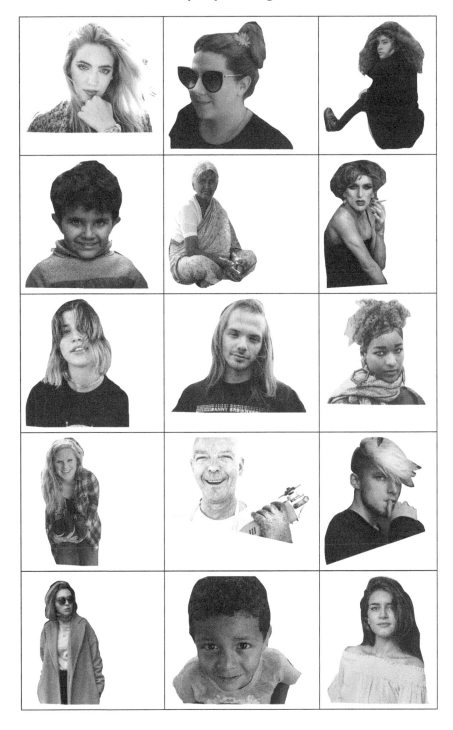

Activity 8: Friendship circle

Purpose: To unpack the meaning of friendship, recognise the boundaries that we create, and illustrate that we can develop deep friendships with those beyond our regular peer group.

Materials: *Friendship layers* worksheet (printable handouts available at https://www.routledge.com/9781138305083).

Suggested time for completion: 30–40 minutes.

Introduction

We often interact with many people during the day. Some are very close to us – those whom we share all our thoughts and feelings with. Others are more distant – acquaintances we interact with, or strangers we see but know little about. When you think about your "friends", who do you include? Are they closer to you or include those who are more distant?

This activity helps students explicitly identify how they see different peers that they interact with, bringing to light the boundaries that are implicitly drawn. For those struggling to feel connected, it can help them realise how many people are around them. For more connected students, it can help them consider ways they implicitly classify others and the impact that it has on their thoughts, behaviours, and feelings. It also challenges students to consider others outside of their peer group who might still be considered a friend – and the role that person might play in their life.

Instructions

Distribute the *Friendship layers* worksheet (on page 85; printable handouts available at https://www.routledge.com/9781138305083). Note that we can think of our different friends as a series of layers. Some are closer to us, some are more distant. We might feel really close to some, whereas others are more distant – but they are still people that we interact with, can learn from and give to. Ask students to consider the circles and think of people that symbolises each circle based on the following description:

- Inner circle: People you consider to be close friends. You have known each other for a long time and feel a deep sense of intimacy and trust.
- Layer 2: People who you are friends with. You speak to them most days. You enjoy their company. If you wanted to hang out with people in the school holidays, this person or people would be included. But you don't share all your thoughts and feelings.
- Layer 3: These are people who you may have known a long time, but you don't see all the time. They could be family friends, or peers that you see during the week and connect with regularly, but are not particularly close.

- Layer 4: These are people who you interact with on occasions through your social groups, hobbies or interests. You might not go to the same school or be in the same year level, but connect through your activities and interests.
- Layer 5: These are people who you do not see every day, but when you do, you always look and smile. You may want to get to know these individuals better if given the opportunity.

Give students 5–10 minutes to fill out the worksheet, adding names that represent each layer.

Next, invite students to join with two peers and share a few of their classifications, giving reasons for why they placed them there. Bringing the group back together, ask a few volunteers to share what they wrote and why.

Finally, debrief with a few questions for reflection:

- Have you ever said that you don't have friends? Why?
- Were you surprised to see how many friends you do have?
- What insights can you gain by considering where different people are in your circle?
- Are there some people that you would like to have closer? What steps could you take to bring them closer into your circle?

Friendship layers

Think about the various friends, peers, and people that you interact with each day and through the week. Who do you consider your close friends? Who is more distant? Fill in names at each layer:

- Inner circle: Those you consider to be close friends. You have known each other for a long time and feel a deep sense of intimacy and trust.
- Layer 2: People who you are friends with. You speak to them most days and enjoy their company, but don't share all your thoughts and feelings with them.
- Layer 3: Those who you may have known a long time, but you don't see all the time. You connect with them regularly, but don't feel particularly close.
- Layer 4: Those who you interact with on occasions through your social groups, hobbies or interests. You connect through your activities, but not beyond that.
- Layer 5: Those who you rarely see, but when you do you always look and smile.

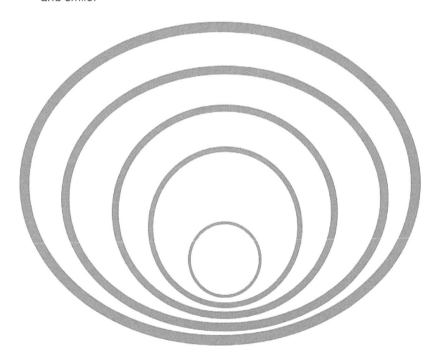

Figure 3.2 Friendship Layers

Module wrap up: Suggested questions for personal reflection or discussion

1   What are some ways that you can show tolerance and acceptance to your peers?
2   How do you manage when someone has a different perspective to your own?
3   What are some things you can do to support, include or help others who are not necessarily within your direct friendship group?

Final thoughts

Peer relationships are important. The activities in this module focus on raising awareness about other's perspectives, learning to value others, and thinking about what students can do to proactively develop good relationships with others. Still, victimization, bullying, relational aggression, and other negative behaviours may still exist. While developing skills to be aware of and connect with others, problems still need to be dealt with. It is important to consider whether there are real barriers affecting social skills and interpersonal relationships. You might like to consider what information you can collect from teachers, parents, and other peers (where appropriate). Or you may consider if referral to an external psychologist is necessary.

References

Allen, K., Kern, P., Vella-Brodrick, D., & Hattie, J., & Waters, L., (2018). What schools need to know about belonging: A meta-analysis. *Educational Psychology Review, 30*(1), 1–34. doi: 10.1007/s10648-016-9389-8

Brown, R., & Evans, W. P. (2002). Extracurricular activity and ethnicity: Creating greater school connection among diverse student populations. *Urban Education, 37*(1), 41–58. doi: 10.1177/0042085902371004

Diener, E. (2000). Subjective well-being: The science of happiness, and a proposal for national index. *American Psychologist, 55*, 34–43.

Eccles, J., & Gootman, J. (2002). *Community programs to promote youth development.* National Research Council and Institute of Medicine. Washington, DC: National Centre for Educational Statistics.

Hamm, J. V., & Faircloth, B. S. (2005). The role of friendship in adolescents' sense of school belonging. *New Directions for Child and Adolescent Development, 2005*(107), 61–78. doi: 10.1002/cd.121

Libbey, H. P. (2004). Measuring student relationships to school: Attachment, bonding, connectedness, and engagement. *Journal of School Health, 74*(7), 275–283.

Myers, D. G. (2000). The funds, friends, and faith of happy people. *American Psychologist, 55*(1), 56–67. http://dx.doi.org/10.1037/0003-066X.55.1.56

Roffey, S., & Boyle, C. (2018). Belief, belonging and the role of schools in reducing the risk of home-grown extremism. In K. Allen & C. Boyle (Eds), *Pathways to Belonging: School belonging in adolescents.* Rotterdam, The Netherlands: BRILL.

Rubin, C., Rubenstein, J. L., Stechler, G., Heeren, T., Halton, A., Housman, D., & Kasten, L. (1992). Depressive affect in "normal" adolescents: Relationship to life stress, family, and friends. *American Journal of Orthopsychiatry, 62*(3), 430–441. http://dx.doi.org/10.1037/h0079352

The Blind Men and the Elephant. Retrieved from www.jainworld.com/literature/story25.htm

Ueno, K. (2005). The effects of friendship networks on adolescent depressive symptoms. *Social Science Researc, 34*(3), 484–510.

Vaquera, E., & Kao, G. (2008). Do you like me as much as I like you? Friendship reciprocity and its effects on school outcomes among adolescents. *Social Science Research, 37*(1), 55–72.

4   Connecting with oneself

I feel happy after I play sport and this helps me have a more positive mood for the rest of the day.

~ Sam, age 13

Module at a glance

In brief

This module highlights the influence of personal characteristics and self-worth to a student's sense of school belonging. It includes activities that encourage optimism and positive sense of identity.

Learning outcomes

- Identify the factors that influence one's identity and sense of self.
- Assess involvement within the school community.
- Use own strengths and optimism to connect and improve relationship with others.

Contents

A case study: Narcissistic or self-assured?

A phone call came in from Hattie's mother, Bronwyn, who shared her concerns about her daughter's "absence" from the family. When the school psychologist asked for clarification, Bronwyn explained that although Hattie was physically present at meals and other family activities, she was mentally absent. Bronwyn noted that Hattie was always on her smartphone, engrossed in various platforms such as Facebook, Instagram, and Snapchat (often all three at once). She was constantly taking "selfies", uploading photos, and texting.

What concerned Bronwyn was the nature of these photos and texts. The family was well off, and Bronwyn and her husband often treated their children to incredible holiday experiences. While Hattie eagerly photographed the journey, the pictures were inevitably of herself, with little in the way of landmarks or tourist attractions. According to Bronwyn, Hattie would spend hours putting on make-up and preparing the shot to get the right selfie.

The phone call triggered additional conversations with both Bronwyn and Hattie. Hattie noted that she aspired to become a fashion designer. She proclaimed to love make-up, style, and photography, seeing it as a form of self-expression. But her mother scoffed at mention of this, claiming there was no artistic merit in "taking photos of yourself". She was convinced Hattie was well on her way to becoming a full-fledged narcissist.

The conversations became an opportunity to help Bronwyn understand the artistic nature of her daughter. Hattie found that posting the pictures allowed her to play with different styles, identifying what others liked and disliked. She had a healthy level of self-esteem. But the conversations also helped Hattie recognise problematic elements of her social media use, and working with the school psychologist, she was able to develop strategies to not allow technology to pre-empt her relationships with her family and others.

What the research says

If you listen to the media, you can get the idea that young people have all become selfie-taking, mirror-hogging narcissists. Indeed, selfies have become incredibly popular. The past decade has also witnessed a growing number of narcissism diagnoses (Twenge & Campbell, 2009). But these are simply symptoms of deeper problems. Indeed, many selfie-obsessed young people struggle with low or unstable levels of self-esteem.

Developmentally, adolescents are exploring who they are, developing a sense of self. Smartphones and social media have accentuated this at a speed and reach beyond anything ever seen before. Rather than a private exploration amongst friends, various images can be broadcast to the world, gaining immediate feedback on what others like and dislike. Those who otherwise might remain unknown can become overnight celebrities, all objectively counted by the number of likes one receives. The "likes" feel good – it's an external reward, which encourages repeat behaviour.

The problem is that the sense of identity and self-worth become dependent on those external indicators. Self-esteem is built around images and others' responses to those images. Yet what is popular one moment is disregard the next moment, and along with it, the adolescent's sense of self-worth can come crashing down. Like a drug addiction, maintaining one's image can become all-consuming and require more and more time to gain the same sense of fulfilment – creating a fierce negative cycle. It can take on the same significance within a young person's life as other survival needs like food and water.

A sense of self-esteem is certainly important. Higher levels of self-esteem predict better academic performance, good social relationships, mental and physical wellbeing, and school belonging. But research has found that the benefits associated with self-esteem can depend upon what the drivers of the self-esteem are (Branden, 1995). When self-esteem is based on one's image, the grades that one can achieve, the ability to go for nights without sleeping, athletic success, or appearing popular, it becomes a fine line between security and complete self-destruction.

In contrast, a healthy sense of self-esteem is grounded in who one is – accepting both one's personal strengths and weaknesses. It's less about the image that is portrayed, and more about the character of the person within.

Personal characteristics – the social and emotional competencies that one has – are a core part of school belonging. A growing amount of research emphasises the importance of strengths of character – what a person is naturally good at – and bringing those strengths out. Our review of the literature shows that optimism, conscientiousness, self-efficacy, sense of self-worth, and other positive characteristics was one of the greatest correlates of school belonging (Allen, Kern, Vella-Brodrick, Waters, & Hattie, 2018). Others similarly find the positive impact of personal characteristics (e.g., Kia-Keating & Ellis, 2007; Reschly, Huebner, Appleton, & Antaramian, 2008; Ryzin, Gravely, & Roseth, 2009; Samdal, Nutbeam, Wold, & Kannas, 1998; Sirin & Rogers-Sirin, 2004; Uwah, McMahon, & Furlow, 2008). Other studies find that positive personal characteristics relate to sociability, social skills, and school engagement (e.g., Connell and Wellborn, 1991; Samdal, Nutbeam, Wold, & Kannas, 1998; Sirin & Rogers-Sirin, 2004). This research suggests that social and emotional learning should be an important priority for schools.

Too often, it is easy to focus on the weaknesses we see and be critical of younger generations. Everyone has strengths, and research suggests that there is benefit in teaching young people how to recognise, value, and use their strengths for the benefit of themselves and others.

Module overview

The Collaborative for Academic, Social, and Emotional Learning (CASEL), one of the leading organisations promoting social and emotional learning, conceptualises social and emotional competencies across five areas (Weissberg, Durlak, Domitrovich, & Gullotta, 2015):

1   *Self-awareness*, recognising emotions and thoughts, assessing personal strengths and limitations as well as possessing a sense of confidence and optimism
2   *Self-management*, regulating emotions through abilities such as productive coping skills and goal setting
3   *Social awareness*, empathising with others and understanding social norms
4   *Relationship skills*, establishing healthy relationships through social skills
5   *Responsible decision-making*, making considered choices about behaviour.

Developing these five areas are core to developing the positive characteristics that support school belonging. The activities in this module aim to help develop some of these skills; we've noted below which areas each activity targets (for more ideas, see https://casel.org/). The activities can be used with individual students or with groups/ classes.

Activity 1: The toilet paper challenge

Purpose: To help students identify their own strengths and to help you get to know each student's strengths and personalities.

Materials: Roll of toilet paper.

Suggested time for completion: 30–40 minutes.

Introduction

This activity encourages students to think about their own strengths and connect with one another through stories, using a tactile modality. When done in a group, it can cause some laughs, as well as provide insights into the strengths and personalities of classmates and peers.

Some students may struggle to identify strengths that they have. Often, we can be quick to see and describe our negative attributes, but have a harder time identifying our strengths. This is called a *negativity bias*, we are biased toward seeing and focusing on negative things rather than positive things. This is one of the reasons that we need to practice seeing strengths in ourselves and others. A benefit of the group activities is that other students can help a young person see strengths they may have overlooked.

This activity allows students to do just that – identifying strengths in themselves and allowing others to identify strengths in them. The activity encourages *self-awareness, social awareness*, and *relationship skills*.

Instructions

For this activity, you need a roll of toilet paper. Pass the roll around, asking students to pull off some toilet paper, taking as much or as little as they'd like, without saying what this is for. Some students will take one or two pieces. Others will take a handful. In fact, there might even be a small competition to take the most (have extra rolls on hand, just in case). This will be funny later on when it is revealed what the toilet paper is for.

Next, have students count the number of pieces they have. Have them report back, finding out who has the most. Then, the purpose of the paper is revealed. Students are to say or describe a positive strength, attribute, talent, or something they are proud of – one per each square of toilet paper. Give the students a few minutes to think, then go around the room and have them share.

If you are only working with one student, take multiple pieces as a model, and encourage them to take more than one square. If working with a group, if students hesitate to take the roll, then tear off some pieces as an example then pass it on (just remember that you will have to share about yourself – equal to the number of pieces you tear off!).

Depending on the size of the group and how much paper students tear off, time might become an issue. In this case, have students share up to five strengths, then move on. Or, bounce around and have some students share, and encourage those without a chance to speak to share their responses with one another at a later time.

Some students may struggle to mention or even think about strengths that they have. If a student struggles, open it up to the group to have others share a strength or positive attribute of the student. You can also discuss this and normalise the experience at the end, noting that often we can be quick to see and describe our negative attributes, but have a harder time identifying our strengths – this is a good reason to practice seeing strengths in ourselves and others.

Activity 2: Layers of influence

Purpose: To help students understand the factors that influence their identity.

Materials: *Layers of influence* worksheet (below; full colour printable hand-outs are recommended and available at https://www.routledge.com/9781138305083).

Suggested time for completion: 30–40 minutes.

Introduction

Adolescence is a period of determining one's identity, sense of self, and place in the world. A lot of factors can impact identity, including one's cultural background, social class, the local community, family and friends, the school, and various experiences in life. While at times we are aware of these various influencers, we often forget that they are there and the impact they can have on our thoughts, emotions, and behaviours.

This activity challenges students to consider different people, experiences, and other things that impact who they are as a person and how their life has unfolded over time. It can also provide you greater insights into the students' lives, better informed to help them to better adjust to their needs moving forward. This activity helps develop *self-awareness*, with some consideration of *responsible decision-making*.

Instructions

Begin by introducing the idea of circles of influence that impact us. On a poster or the front board, create an image of multiple nested circles, like in the worksheet below. Allow the group to come up with examples at each level (have some ideas in mind in case they get stuck – see the Introduction– this activity uses a simpler version of the Rainbow Model of School Belonging and the examples given in the worksheet). Then have the students complete the *Layers of influence* worksheet (below; full colour printable handouts available at https://www.routledge.com/9781138305083 and are recommended). The students might work on this individually or in small groups of two or three. Bring the group back together and discuss any insights gained as they worked through the activity.

If working with an individual, talk through the task, giving a few examples at each level. Have the student complete the sheet, providing ideas if they get stuck. Then, discuss insights gained as they worked through the sheet.

Building off the final comment on the worksheet ("Sometimes we can control the things around us, sometimes we can't. But by becoming more aware of what makes us who we are, it can help us to take control of our lives, changing the things that we can and accepting the things that we cannot"), end with a discussion around how understanding these different layers of influence can help us be more responsible for how we think, act, and feel. Some students are prone to blaming others for their actions and need to learn to take responsibility for their own actions. Others blame themselves for things beyond their control and need to learn that not everything is their fault. Consider with the students how understanding the positive and negative factors that are more or less under their control can help them be establish a healthy level of responsibility.

Layers of influence

Do you ever think about why you are the way that you are? Some is based on your genes – what you inherited from your mum and dad. Perhaps you are tall or short, perhaps you have brown or blue or hazel eyes, perhaps your skin colour is lighter or darker.

But what about other parts of you? What are your likes and dislikes? Who do you typically hang out with? What makes you who you are? How did you get to be the person you are?

There's heaps of things that impact who we are, the experiences that we have, and our ways of thinking and behaving. We can think about it like layers of an onion:

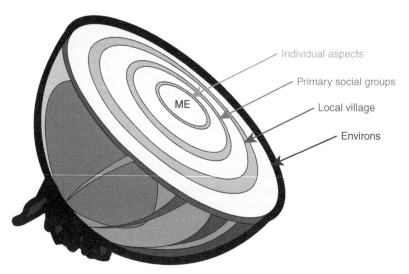

Figure 4.1 An onion representing the layers of influences in our lives.

You are at the core of the onion, but that core is impacted by different layers around it. At the closest layer, there are **individual aspects**. Are you a social butterfly or do you prefer to spend time on your own? Do you get upset easily or do you tend to be happy and easy going? Do you like things ordered and predictable, or do you prefer spontaneity? We all have different personalities, talents, strengths, weaknesses, likes, dislikes, etc. When we think about who we are, these are often the things that we think of first.

But these aren't the only things that impact how we think, feel, and behave. Beyond individual factors, we are impacted by our **primary social groups**. This refers to the people that are a part of our lives – parents and family members, friends, peers, and teachers. For example, if a friend gives you a gift, it probably makes you feel good, but if a friend invites other friends over and leaves you out, it probably makes you feel sad. You are the same person, but how you feel depends on your friend's action.

Then there's the **local village**. This refers to the communities that you are a part of – the school environment, where you live, what your neighbours are like. Then there's **environs** – things like the country that you live in, your cultural background, the local laws, the political system, and the natural environment. We have less control over these factors, but it still impacts who we are, how we think, and our experiences in life.

Often, we don't recognise all the things around us that have an impact on us. This activity identifies some of the things that influence us.

First, take a moment and think about the things that impact on you at each level. Consider these questions to give you some ideas:

- **Individual aspects:** What words would you use to describe yourself? What are your strengths and talents? How well do you cope with stress? What do you enjoy doing?
- **Primary social groups:** What are the important relationships in your life? Are you close to your mum or dad? Do you have siblings? Do you see other family members? Who are your close friends? Do your teachers know you well? Who do you relate with on a daily or weekly basis?
- **Local village:** What's your community and neighbourhood like? Are people friendly or unfriendly? Is it clean and orderly, or is there often rubbish and graffiti around? Do people walk or cycle a lot, or do people drive everywhere? Are there stores and restaurants around? What's your school like?
- **Environs:** Do you live in the city or the countryside? What's the local culture like? What historical factors have impacted your community? What is the political system? Is religion common or uncommon? What languages are spoken?

Now, in the table below, list several things at each level that have an impact on you. Include as many as you can think of (use the back of the page if needed).

Individual	

Primary social groups	
Local village	
Environs	

Finally, in the table, **circle** the things that have a **positive influence** on you and **place a rectangle** around the things that have a **negative influence** on you. How many positives and negatives are there?

Sometimes we can control the things around us, sometimes we can't. But by becoming more aware of what makes us who we are, it can help us to take control of our lives, changing the things that we can and accepting the things that we cannot.

Activity 3: Welcome to Zoolog

Purpose: To help students build self-awareness and to value their own strengths.

Materials: Pen and paper.

Suggested time for completion: 20–30 minutes.

Introduction

If you've ever moved to a new town or country, it can be scary and challenging to start over in a new place, get to know others in the community, and establish yourself. Shifting cultures makes us acutely aware of who we are and how we fit – or don't fit – with those around us.

This activity focuses on building *self-awareness*. It uses an analogy of arriving to a new planet to help students think about who they are, and how they want to be seen. It aims to strip away existing expectations of friends, teachers, and parents, helping them to be themselves. It can also provide insights into how young people sees themselves, their background, and who they want to be.

Instructions

Students can complete this on their own or in pairs. Say to the students:

> Imagine that you move to the imaginary planet of Zoolog. To become an official register, you must go through a screening process, in which you are asked to describe yourself. What would you say? What are your unique characteristics? Have you had special experiences or do you have certain needs that Zoolog needs to be aware of? What's your family and extended family like? Are you bringing along family and friends or coming on your own? Do you speak a foreign language? Do you have pets? What are your favourite activities, your favourite holiday, and how do you like to spend a holiday? What strengths will you bring to the Zoolog community?
>
> Provide the Zoolog officials with as much information as you can about what makes you distinct from others and consider the significance of what you want Zoolog to know about. Think as broadly as you can and be creative, but also be realistic, staying true to yourself. Remember, no one in Zoolog knows who you are – all they will know is what you tell them.

Bring the students back together and ask for some volunteers to share their description. Ask how they felt about constructing their description. What difference did it make in thinking about an imaginary world, versus their everyday life? Discuss with the students how stepping away from typical constraints (like expectations of friends and families) can help us think about who we are, who we want to be, and what makes us special. Reflect on lessons learned through the activity.

Activity 4: Creating my best possible future

Purpose: To help students be optimistic about the future and to identify pathways to turn their goals and ambitions into reality.

Materials: *My best possible future* worksheet (printable handouts available at https://www.routledge.com/9781138305083).

Suggested time for completion: 30–40 minutes.

Introduction

In our review of the research, a strong correlate of school belonging was having a sense of hope and optimism. It's hard to be motivated in your school work when all you see is a bleak future ahead of you. Optimistic individuals imagine a bright future. They believe that there are good things to come in the future, and that things will work out, even if there are challenges along the way.

However, optimism is not just positive thinking – blindly believing that all will work out. Rather, optimistic individuals have a positive vision of the future, and then identify specific actions they can take to bring that future about. The literature indicates that hopeful individuals set specific goals and make plans to bring those goal about (Snyder, 1994). They identify some alternatives, so if plan A doesn't work out, there's always plan B (what the literature calls *pathway thinking*, or *waypower*). They also maintain an "I can do it" attitude (what the literature calls *self-efficacy* or *willpower*). Thus, hope and optimism involve identifying a positive dream, identifying ways to bring that dream about and maintaining a sense of being able to do so.

In the positive psychology literature, a popular activity is the "best possible self" (King, 2001). The idea is to imagine yourself in the future, with the best possible life you can imagine. Some students find this easy – they have a clear vision of how they want their life to go. Others have not thought about the future, and this can open their imagination of what could be. Other students find this challenging. They may have a bleak view of the future, and have trouble imagining things being better. This activity aims to ignite a sense of hope.

Beyond identifying a positive vision for the future, this activity also helps students start to identify several pathways they can take to make that dream a reality, as well as think about ways to stay motivated along the way – building the social-emotional skill of *self-management*. The activity includes a period of self-reflection along with peer-coaching to consider pathways forward.

Instructions

Begin by giving students the following instructions:

> Close your eyes. Imagine that you are 25-years-old, and you have exactly the life that you want. All has worked out, even better than you could have imagined is possible. Take a moment and think about what your life looks like.

Give students a few minutes to think, then hand out the *My best possible future* worksheet (below; printable handouts available at https://www.routledge.com/9781138305083). Instruct them to focus on the top part of the page. Give students 10–15 minutes to write about the future they imagine.

Next, have students pair up. One person will act as the coach, the other as the coachee, and then switch roles.

1 Share your vision with your partner.
2 Ask your partner:

- How can you bring that future about (what is a pathway you can follow? What are other possibilities?)
- How will you stay motivated (what personal resources will you draw on? How can others help you?)
- How can I help?

Next, give students 5–10 minutes to record their thoughts and insights on the bottom portion of the worksheet.

Bring students together and invite several students to share their dreams and their ideas on how to turn that into reality. Encourage those who share, no matter how simple or unrealistic the dream is. Ask other students how they can support one another in their journeys.

If you are working with an individual, have the student describe what they wrote, and work with them to create a realistic plan, with a clear next step. Identify who can support them as they move forward (e.g., parents, a teacher, a friend).

Emphasise the importance of both having dreams for the future, as well as realistic pathways forward. Remind students to keep believing that their dreams are possible – we can do much more than we think, if we are only willing to try.

My best possible future

Take a few minutes and think about your dreams for the future. Imagine that you are 25 years old, and you have exactly the life that you want. All has worked out, even better than you could have imagined is possible. Now, write about what you imagined. You might describe your day, or what your life looks like. Or are you married or living alone? Do you have kids? What work do you do? What have you achieved? What activities do you do? Include as many details as possible.

What insights came from your partner discussion? Think about what is needed to make that vision a reality. What is needed? What skills do you need to develop? What resources can help you along the way? What's a first step that you can take towards making that vision a reality?

Activity 5: Goal setting for personal growth

Purpose: To help students recognise the social and emotional skills they could develop further and set relevant SMART goals for personal growth.

Materials: *Developing growth goals* worksheet (below and printable handouts available at https://www.routledge.com/9781138305083).

Suggested time for completion: 45–60 minutes.

Introduction

When we think about goal setting at school, students often think about academic goals, such as getting into a certain university or profession, graduating, earning a certain grade, passing an exam, mastering a topic, or completing a maths assignment. Other goals might focus on sports (e.g., run 1 km), health (eat healthy foods), or social goals (I will get 10,000 likes on my Instagram post). It is less common for students to set goals related to their personal attributes, such as coping skills ("I will cope better with stress"), responsible decision-making, and social awareness.

Goals are important for motivating behaviour – especially when those goals are SMART (specific, measurable, achievable, realistic, and timely). Setting and pursuing personal goals related to social and emotional competencies, pro-social pursuits and self-care can help students proactively manage their own mental health and wellbeing.

This activity begins by having students reflect on the value of setting goals (questions adapted from the California Healthy Kids Survey, 2007/2008; Kern, Benson, Steinberg, & Steinberg, 2016; and Nese et al., 2012). They next consider the personal competencies that they do well, and which ones they could improve upon. They then identify one or two areas that they could develop further. Working in small groups, students will be asked to set SMART personal competency goals, and begin thinking about how to reach that goal. The activity targets *self-awareness* and *self-management* skills. It also helps students practise thinking about what SMART goals are.

Instructions

Begin by asking students about some of the short-term and long-term goals that they have. Then, note the following:

Have you ever thought about setting wellbeing goals? We might say "I want to be happy", but what does that actually mean?

One way to start building our wellbeing is by developing personal and social competencies – skills for understanding ourselves and others well, managing your thoughts, emotions, and behaviours, and improving your relationships with others. In the same way we have academic and other types of goals, we can set goals related to our own personal growth and development.

But goals are more likely to be met if they are SMART goals. What might be some examples of SMART goals?

[If students are unfamiliar with SMART goals, introduce these and consider some examples.]

Provide students with the *Developing growth goals* worksheet (below; printable handouts available at https://www.routledge.com/9781138305083). Give them a few minutes to individually complete Section 1: evaluating their areas of strengths and weaknesses, selecting one or two areas to focus on, and noting any ideas on relevant goals they could set.

Invite students to form groups of three to four students. Depending on comfort levels, they might join with friends or peers they know well, or they may prefer to work with less known peers. One person should share the area they want to focus on, and the group should brainstorm possible goals. Encourage students to consider which goals might be SMARTer than others. Allow time for each student to share and gather ideas from their group, noting ideas down in Section 2 of the worksheet.

Finally, give students a few minutes for personal reflection. Taking the ideas generated from the group and their own thoughts, identify a SMART personal competency goal, along with some ideas on how to start pursuing that goal, noting their goal and a few steps they can take to start pursuing that goal in Section 3 of the worksheet.

Developing growth goals

In this activity, you will be asked to reflect on your own personal competencies, select an area to focus on, and develop a SMART goal to proactively start developing that area.

Section 1

Below are a series of statements and the skill area they relate to. Read each statement and tick the square that best reflects whether this is something you do very well, moderately well, or not well at all. There are no right or wrong answers.

	Statement and response	Skill
1	I deal with stress ☐ Not very well ☐ Moderately well ☐ Very well	Stress management
2	I have ways to cope when things go wrong ☐ Not very well ☐ Moderately well ☐ Very well	Coping
3	I feel well-balanced emotionally ☐ Not very well ☐ Moderately well ☐ Very well	Emotional stability
4	I work hard ☐ Not very well ☐ Moderately well ☐ Very well	Persistence
5	I generally feel happy ☐ Not very well ☐ Moderately well ☐ Very well	Happiness
6	I am reliable – others can trust that I will do what I say I will do ☐ Not very well ☐ Moderately well ☐ Very well	Reliability
7	I believe that things will work out, no matter how difficult they seem ☐ Not very well ☐ Moderately well ☐ Very well	Optimism

8	I understand my moods and feelings	Self-awareness
	☐ Not very well ☐ Moderately well ☐ Very well	
9	I am able to understand how other people feel and think	Social awareness
	☐ Not very well ☐ Moderately well ☐ Very well	
10	I am flexible and adaptable, able to shift when things change	Flexibility
	☐ Not very well ☐ Moderately well ☐ Very well	
11	I take responsibility for my own thoughts, feelings, and behaviours	Responsibility
	☐ Not very well ☐ Moderately well ☐ Very well	
12	I care about what happens to other people	Caring for others
	☐ Not very well ☐ Moderately well ☐ Very well	
13	I stand up for myself without putting others down	Positive assertiveness
	☐ Not very well ☐ Moderately well ☐ Very well	
14	I know how to calm down when I am stressed or upset	Emotion regulation
	☐ Not very well ☐ Moderately well ☐ Very well	
15	I am good at having conversations with other people	Communication
	☐ Not very well ☐ Moderately well ☐ Very well	
16	I feel bad when someone gets their feelings hurt	Empathy
	☐ Not very well ☐ Moderately well ☐ Very well	
17	I know where to go for help if I have a problem	Help-seeking
	☐ Not very well ☐ Moderately well ☐ Very well	

18	I feel close to people at my school	School connection
	☐ Not very well ☐ Moderately well ☐ Very well	
19	There are many things I do well	Self-efficacy
	☐ Not very well ☐ Moderately well ☐ Very well	
20	I get along well with my teachers	Teacher connection
	☐ Not very well ☐ Moderately well ☐ Very well	
21	I'm good at connecting with my peers	Peer connection
	☐ Not very well ☐ Moderately well ☐ Very well	
22	I'm interested in the work and activities at school	School engagement
	☐ Not very well ☐ Moderately well ☐ Very well	
23	I take initiative to get tasks done	Initiative
	☐ Not very well ☐ Moderately well ☐ Very well	
24	I'm good at working in a group or team	Teamwork
	☐ Not very well ☐ Moderately well ☐ Very well	
25	I listen carefully to what others say	Listening
	☐ Not very well ☐ Moderately well ☐ Very well	

Personal reflection questions

Which areas are your strengths (where you checked that you do this "very well"?

Which areas are your weaknesses (where you checked "not very well")?

Of the areas that you are weaker at, pick one to focus on. What's a goal that you could set to develop this? Be ready to share this with your group.

After you complete this section, wait for further instructions.

Section 2

What ideas does your group have? Take notes as others brainstorm ideas. Place a star next to or circle SMART goals.

Section 3

Reflect on the ideas from your group. What's a SMART personal competency goal you can pursue? What are one or two small things you can do to start pursuing that goal?

Activity 6: A change of plans

Purpose: To help students value creating plans, but also be flexible about changing plans along the way.

Materials: None.

Suggested time for completion: 30–60 minutes.

Introduction

Do you like to create and follow a detailed plan, or do you prefer spontaneity? Whether you like them or not, plans play an important role in helping us reach the goals that we hope to achieve. Planning involves thinking ahead, considering what might happen and the best route to get there. It also motivates behaviour – especially as we get excited about what we plan to do. Several of the other activities in this module include planning as a core component to reaching goals.

However, even the best plans can fall apart. Someone gets sick, the weather shifts, you get a flat tyre. Such changes can be stressful and unsettling, but occur quite often. This activity helps students to recognise that plans can and do change, identify ways to be flexible when plans need to change, and recognise the impact that changing plans can have on others. This activity focuses especially on developing *self-management*, along with some aspects of *relationship skills* and *responsible decision making*.

Instructions

First, reflect on the value of developing plans, especially for achieving goals that we want to achieve. Ask students to take a moment to thinking about some of the plans they have made in the past. Then read the following scenario:

> Amelia and her bestie, Fiona, have been planning an amazing holiday. Both of the girls have saved up as much money as they could, spent time planning the trip at the travel agent, and choosing incredible activities to do in their dream destination.
>
> Now Amelia is on the phone with Fiona, a week before they are due to leave. Amelia is so excited about the upcoming trip. As she's about to sort out some final details, Fiona cuts in, noting that there is a change of plans. She explains that she has an important interview scheduled at the time they are supposed to be away, and that she can't miss the interview. She states quite bluntly that the trip will need to be postponed or cancelled. Amelia feels hurt and angry.

Demonstrate a role play. Have one student play Fiona and one act as Amelia. What does Amelia do? How does Fiona react?

Our natural reaction when plans are changed or disappointment occurs can be quite negative. Discuss with the students:

How do you think Amelia felt when she heard the news? Was this true in this scenario? How did Amelia's response impact Fiona? What was the result for Amelia and Fiona? How can Amelia negotiate the change in plans? Might there be some alternatives? What about a compromise?

Then, have students pair up or join groups of up to four. Invite them to play out the scene, switching roles and playing out different reactions on the part of Amelia and Fiona. If you have groups of three or four, have other students watch the scenario as an observer and provide advice and suggestions to Fiona and Amelia, acting as mediators.

Come back together and discuss the experience:

What was it like to alter your plans? What was the result?

Plans are important − they help direct and motivate our behaviour. They can help us be excited about what's to come and help us reach our goals. But at times, plans have to change − and dealing with change can be really hard. We might feel let down and as a result, we feel angry or sad. Those feelings are valid. But how we manage those feeling can make a big difference in the results. If someone changes plans on you, it can be helpful to take a few deep breaths before responding. If you feel really angry, sometimes it's better to walk away for a little bit to cool down.

When you do make plans with others, also consider how changing plans might affect them. The other person might feel very angry or sad about the change. Think about how you can communicate any changes in a kind way, accept any emotional responses, and be open to considering possible compromises or alternative solutions.

Invite students to share any final thoughts and reflections.

Activity 7: Pictures of my life at school

Purpose: To help students assess and make sense of their involvement within the school community.

Materials: Camera or smartphone with a camera, pen and paper (or computer for writing stories).

Suggested time for completion: 5-minute intro, 1-week assignment, 20-minute follow-up.

Introduction

Schools offer a wide range of groups and activities − music and creative arts, sport, academic activities and special competitions, debating, leadership . . . the list is endless. Groups and activities at school provide a great opportunity for students to connect and feel a part of the school. They can provide a sense of confidence and self-worth. They often require students to follow social norms, be aware of others, and develop positive relational skills. They require that students manage time effectively. Together, they help students learn how to become a contributing member of society – an important skill to develop through adolescence (Kern, Park, Peterson, & Romer, 2017). Thus, groups provide numerous opportunities to develop *self-awareness, self-management, social awareness, relationship skills*, and *responsible decision making*.

Some students are very much involved in groups and activities, enjoying being an active part of the school community. Others are involved in everything, but feel stressed about trying to fit everything in. Others are happy with one or two activities or are involved in clubs and activities outside of school. And some are disengaged with groups or activities, perhaps because they are completely focused on school work alone, don't get along with others involved in the activities, or have no interest in what is offered.

This activity encourages students to consider how they fit into the school community, and to create a narrative around what life at school beyond the classroom means to them. Depending on the student, this activity can serve several purposes:

- Given that the amount of active involvement in activities and groups at school vary from student to student, this activity can help students incorporate their activities into part of their narrative and social identity and inspire motivated students to continue staying active and involved.
- Some students might feel somewhat disconnected, but are actually much more involved than they realise. This activity can help students identify all the group activities they are involved in at school, identify the ways that they fit within the school, highlight and help them appreciate aspects of school life that they otherwise might take for granted.
- Some students are overly involved in groups and activities and would benefit from doing fewer activities well. This activity can help them evaluate what they are involved in at school. Of their activities, which resonate with them, and which might they be better focusing on?
- Some students are involved in few or no activities at school, but are well connected outside of school. This activity can help students see how their life inside and outside of school intersect and can be mutually supportive.
- Some students are quite disconnected from the school and groups outside of school. Such students are at the highest risk of disconnection from the school. This activity can first identify the need for connection, as well as highlight aspects of school life that the young person might be interested in connecting to. For such students, it's important to validate feelings of disconnection, but use this as an opportunity for connecting groups with interests and strengths, rather than as a judgment on a lack of involvement or triggering additional feelings that they don't belong.

This activity takes very little preparation and you can adjust the time based on what is available. As students often are involved in different activities through the week, it works best with introducing the activity at one session, giving students a week to work, and then reporting back at the next session.

Instructions

Begin by asking students about some of the groups or activities that they are involved in – mostly at school, but also outside of school. Have a few students share why they are involved in their groups and how it makes them feel (guide them towards responses such as the group being fun, provides friends, et cetera.)

Say to the student(s):

> What is your life at school like? This activity helps you to create a visual representation of your life at school. Over the next week, your goal is to create a visual representation of the groups and activities that you are involved in, at school and beyond. Take pictures of the activities at school that are meaningful to you, places that you hang out at, and groups you are a part of. Alternatively, you can take pictures of activities and groups that you wish you were a part of. You can choose what to include, although please make sure all images are appropriate to share.
>
> Next, write about your photos. You might tell a story of what you do in your groups and how they connect to you as a person. You may also like to give a brief description of what each photo represents and why you included it. Bring your stories and photos back to the group or class next week.

At the next session, place students into groups of three to five (preferably with peers beyond their close friends) and invite students to share their pictures and stories. By sharing in groups, they can find connections with others in the group, and also get ideas of other things to be involved in. Walk around and listen in, gaining your own insights into what the school looks like from their perspective.

Finally, bring the groups back together. Ask a few students to share some of their pictures and descriptions. Reflect with the students on any insights gained through the activity.

After the session, follow up with any students that found the activity uncomfortable or appeared disconnected to activities and groups at school.

If you are working with an individual student, have the student create their story over the week, and then talk through their pictures and tell their story with you. If the student is able to demonstrate they are well connected, validate the activities, noting how great that involvement is. Consider if every activity is a good fit, or if the student might consider putting more energy into some places and letting go of others (without letting go of school work!).

If a student shows signs of being disconnected, you might consider with them what their photos show. What do they long to be a part of? Using goal setting approaches (see Activity 7 in this module for ideas), develop a goal for connecting with one of the interests shown, and develop a plan to make that a reality. Include very small steps. Follow up with the student to encourage them to follow that plan.

Activity 8: The unknown and alone

Purpose: To help normalise anxieties and challenges of school, reducing fears of the unknown and feeling alone in one's struggles.

Materials: None.

Suggested time for completion: 20–60 minutes, over one or more sessions.

Introduction

A source of anxiety and feelings of stress can come from *the unknown* – what to expect in an unknown situation – and *the alone* – the feeling that you are the only one struggling. School can contain a lot of unknowns. When we don't know what to expect, we create our own expectations or what might happen. For some students, this envisioned future is quite positive. But many see that unknown as negative and threatening. At an extreme, some students imagine worse case scenarios. Images of what could happen play out in their mind, leading to what can become paralysing anxiety. Such feelings can be very isolating – especially when others seemingly are fine (even though they might be hiding similar feelings) and can affect their sense of school belonging.

There can be great value in learning from those who have walked the road before us. While each person has their own journey through school, stories from others can tell us more about what we might expect, helping us to look forward to the good things, and be mentally prepared for the hard things. Knowing others went through similar experiences and had similar emotions can make what seems impossible more possible. It can also help us not feel so alone when we have such feelings. For example, when we feel anxious about having to do a class project with an unknown group, we can learn to recognise those feelings are normal, allowing us to take a deep breath and plunge forward, rather than being crippled by fears of what could happen.

In an interesting series of studies led by Greg Walton and colleagues from Stanford University, he primarily worked with university students, from a range of ethnic backgrounds and representing different gender groups, who had been enrolled for several years were recruited to speak to first year students about the difficulties they faced when they first started university (Walton & Brady, 2019; Walton, Murphy, Logel, Yeager, & The College Transition Collaborative, 2017; Yeager et al., 2016). They spoke about the challenges of fitting in, belonging, establishing new friendship groups, common worries and thoughts, and positive and negatives experiences that transitioning from school to university brought. The study found that the first-year students benefited socially and emotionally from the experience. The stories normalised some of the challenging emotions of transitioning to university. They also gained ideas on how to transition well, helping them connect with the university and establish a greater sense of belonging over the months to come. Social-belonging interventions, like the one described above have been found to have a lasting impact on self-esteem, achievement, the ability to manage stress, physical health outcomes, and the amount of friendships formed (Walton & Brady, 2019; Walton et al., 2017; Walton & Cohen, 2011; Yeager et al., 2016).

This activity is a variant of the university study, and targets *social awareness* and *self-management*. It is inspired by Greg Walton's research, but does not detail the actual process or exercise that was tested in his research. In this case, older students visit younger students and share about their experiences, challenges, and victories traversing through school. Younger students benefit from learning from the older students. Year 11 or 12 students might visit Year 7 or 8 students, or you might invite local university students to visit Year 11 and 12s. It can be particularly helpful to include students who struggled at first but developed a sense of belonging over time.

This activity may also be a benefit for the older students who share their story – helping them process the experiences they've had, and also acknowledge the successes they've had – helping them to draw on similar skills in the future.

You might have several students come in at one time, let them share, and discuss their experiences, or include several stories over time, challenging students to consider what they learn from each story. This activity requires a bit more time and energy to set up compared to the other activities in this book, but it can be well worth the effort.

Instructions

Arrange for several older students to visit your group. Ensure that the students you choose are diverse and representative of the different ethnic, cultural, or religious groups at your school. Begin by asking the younger students to share some of the fears that they have about the next few years. What scares them? What worries do they have? The aim of this exercise is for older students to articulate that challenges and difficulties in transition are normal and they can be overcome.

Then ask the older students to share their experiences. You might ask them questions such as:

- How did it feel to start secondary school?
- What were some of the challenges you faced?

- How did you tackle making new friends?
- How did you overcome feelings of not fitting in?
- What helped you to connect to school?
- Have your feelings about school changed since Year 7?
- Why do you now feel a sense of belonging school?

You may also like to open up questions from the younger students.

Once the interviews are over, invite students to reflect on what they have learned, asking questions such as:

- What insights did they learn from the older students?
- How can they apply these insights into your own experiences?
- How can you use these insights to prepare for future challenges or transitions?

Module wrap up: Suggested questions for personal reflection or discussion

1   Think about the information you now have, of who YOU are. How can you apply your strengths to school?
2   What would you like to work on in order to cope more effectively at school?
3   If you had to describe how you belong to school to someone else, what would you say?

Final thoughts

Social and emotional skills are core to developing socially and emotionally competent individuals with a strong sense of self and good relationships with others. The activities throughout this module aim to help students become more aware of themselves and others. This module aims to help students identify strengths, areas to develop, make goals for the future, and develop pathways to move forward. While some students are naturally stronger in some areas than others, all social and emotional competencies can be taught and developed. But they can take time. It can be challenging to confront areas of weakness, and even harder to make change. Still, adolescence is a critical period to be developing such skills.

Throughout the module, we've suggested ways to help students positively connect with and appreciate themselves. For many students, self-awareness can help develop a healthy level of self-esteem. Still, some students struggle a lot with having a positive view of themselves. By mid-adolescence, many are already struggling with poor body image, eating disorders, and other negative behaviours. Such students may require further intensive and ongoing work and should be connected with professional support.

References

Allen, K. A., Kern, P., Vella-Brodrick, D., Waters, L., & Hattie, J. (2018). What schools need to know about belonging: A meta-analysis. *Educational Psychology Review, 30*(1), 1–34. doi: 10.1007/s10648-016-9389-8

Branden, N. (1995). *The six pillars of self-esteem*. New York: Bantam Books.

California Healthy Kids Survey. (2007/2008). California School District secondary school survey results fall 2007/ spring 2008. *California Department of Education.*

Connell, J. P., & Wellborn, J. G. (1991). Competence, autonomy and relatedness: A motivational analysis of self-system processes. In M. R. Gunnar & L. A. Sroufe (Eds), *Minnesota symposium on child psychology, 22* (pp. 43–77). Hillsdale, MI: L. Erlbaum Associates.

Kern, M. L., Benson, L., Steinberg, E. A., & Steinberg, L. (2016). The EPOCH measure of adolescent well-being. *Psychological Assessment, 28*, 586–597.

Kern, M. L., Park, N., Peterson, C., & Romer, D. (2017). The positive perspective on youth development. In D. Romer & the Commission Chairs of the Adolescent Mental Health Initiative of the Annenberg Public Policy Center and the Sunnylands Trust (Eds) *Treating and preventing adolescent mental disorders: What we know and what we don't know* (v. 2) (pp. 543–567). New York: Oxford University Press.

Kia-Keating, M., & Ellis, B. (2007). Belonging and connection to school in resettlement: Young refugees, School belonging, and psychosocial adjustment. *Clinical Child Psychology and Psychiatry, 12*(1), 29–43.

King, L. A. (2001). The health benefits of writing about life goals. *Personality and Social Psychology Bulletin, 27*, 798–807.

Nese, R. N. T., Doerner, E., Romer, N., Kaye, N. C., Merrell, K. W., & Tom, K. M. (2012). Social emotional assets and resilience scales: Development of a strength-based short-form behaviour rating scale system. *Journal of Education Research Online, 4*, 124–139.

Reschly, A. L., Huebner, E. S., Appleton, J. J., & Antaramian, S. (2008). Engagement as flourishing: The contribution of positive emotions and coping to adolescents' engagement at school and with learning. *Psychology in the Schools, 45*(5), 419–431.

Ryzin, M. J., Gravely, A. A., & Roseth, C. J. (2009). Autonomy, belongingness, and engagement in school as contributors to adolescent psychological wellbeing. *Journal of Youth and Adolescence, 38*(1), 1–12.

Samdal, O., Nutbeam, D., Wold, B., & Kannas L. (1998). Achieving health and educational goals through schools: A study of the importance of the climate and students' satisfaction with school. *Health Education Research, 3*, 383–397. doi: 10.1093/her/13.3.383

Sirin, S. R., & Rogers-Sirin, L. (2004). Exploring school engagement of middle-class African American adolescents. *Youth & Society, 35*(3), 323–340.

Snyder, C. R. (1994). *The psychology of hope: You can get there from here*. New York: Free Press.

Twenge, J. M., & Campbell, W. K. (2009). *The narcissism epidemic: Living in the age of entitlement*. New York: Atria Paperback.

Yeager, D. S., Walton, G. M., Brady, S. T., Akcinar, E. N., Paunesku, D., Keane, L., Kamentz, D., . . . & Dweck, C. S. (2016). Teaching a lay theory before college narrows achievement gaps at scale. Proceedings of the National Academy of Sciences of the United States of America, *113*(24), D3341–E3348. http://dx.doi.org/10.1073/pnas.1524360113

Uwah, C., McMahon, G., & Furlow, C. (2008). *School belonging, educational aspirations, and academic self-efficacy among African American male high school students: Implications for school counselors.* Professional School Counseling. Retrieved from http://www.thefreelibrary.com/School+belonging,+educational+aspirations,+and+academic+self-efficacy. . .-a0180860878

Walton, G. M. & Brady, S. T. (2019). The social-belonging intervention. To appear in G. M. Walton & A. Crum (Eds) (2019). *The handbook of wise interventions: how social-psychological insights can help solve problems.* New York, NY: Guilford.

Walton, G. M., Murphy, M. C., Logel, C., Yeager, D. S., & The College Transition Collaborative (2017). *The social-belonging intervention: A guide for use and customization.* Available at: http://collegetransitioncollaborative.org/content/2017/belonging-custom-guide/.

Walton, G. W. & Cohen, G. L. (2011). A brief social-belonging intervention improves academic and health outcomes of minority students. *Science, 331*(6023), 1447–1451

Weissberg, R. P., Durlak, J. A., Domitrovich, C. E., & Gullotta, T. P. (2015). Social and emotional learning: Past, present, and future. In J. A. Durlak, C. E. Domitrovich, R. P. Weissberg, & T. P. Gullotta (Eds) *Handbook of social and emotional learning: Research and practice* (pp. 3–19). New York, NY: Guilford Press.

5 Connecting with learning

I used to think maths was dumb and I would never use it once I finished school. I then met a teacher who made me realise that there is mathematics in nearly everything we do. This made me like maths a lot more.

~ *Brendon, age 16*

Module at a glance

In brief

This module explains the association between academic motivation and school belonging, and provides activities that promote motivation and positive thinking.

Learning outcomes

- Relate the value of school and education with academic goals.
- Create and organise a study routine.
- Recognise the importance of learning from mistakes and positive thinking.

Contents

A case study: A disconnected student

James was first referred to the school psychologist by the school principal, who had received a letter from James' parents advising of James' withdrawal from the school. The reasons for withdrawal were unclear. Under such circumstances, the principal liked to give students an opportunity to talk with the school psychologist about any school-based issues that could possibly be resolved before leaving. Often by the time a school withdrawal letter appears, the family have already made up their mind to change schools and have set up alternative school arrangements, but occasionally it might have been a hasty decision and perceived problems can be remedied. At other times, especially when the discussion is driven by the parents' perception of what might be right for their child, the young person can feel a sense of grief and loss over needing to change schools, a sense of failure at not being able to fit at school, and fear of what's to come. In such cases, the school psychologist can help the young person process the loss and prepare for the transition.

This was not the case for James. He hated school and reported that he had held these feelings for years. James saw his classes as pointless, the topics were uninspiring, the teachers were aloof, and his classmates were dull. He rarely did homework, spending his time engaging in online gaming, reading books of his own choice, and tinkering with electronics. As a result, James wanted to drop out of school. As a compromise, his parents made the decision to change schools, hoping another environment might be a better fit.

A decade earlier, young people could assert their independence by leaving school completely. Studies have clearly demonstrated the value of education for preparing young people for life and as a consequence, the minimum age for leaving school within Australia is now 17 years. Students who choose to leave school prior to this age must do so with good justification and forward planning regarding their educational/vocational pathway. Despite his hatred of school, at 13, James was required by law to continue his education.

The counselling session was a struggle, but the psychologist slowly built rapport. She reminded James that he – like other students who wanted to leave – was welcome to go elsewhere, but that might not necessarily fix things. He might benefit from working with someone at the new school to learn strategies that would help him to find ways to make learning work for him, rather than disconnecting completely.

James changed school and as suspected by the school psychologist, changing the environment did not immediately fix things. James found many similarities of the two school environments. But rather than disconnecting, he visited the school psychologist at the new school, who helped him identify his strengths and talents and connect those with his schoolwork. He learned strategies for engaging more in class, which saw him connect better with teachers and his peers. Classes became more enjoyable, and he became more driven, even doing extra assignments in his maths and computer classes to deepen his understanding of relevant topics.

What the research says

Academic motivation is primarily concerned with how much students are motivated to do well at school (Libbey, 2004). This motivation includes cognitive and behavioural components. Behaviour might be motivated internally, through one's inner drive to learn (i.e., intrinsic motivation) or through more external drivers (i.e., extrinsic motivation) (Ryan & Deci, 2000). Applied to learning, academic motivation involves the ability to plan, set goals and exhibit academic confidence, and can be driven by internal, external, or a combination of internal and external drivers. Greater academic motivation plays an important role in promoting good academic performance.

Our review of the empirical literature found that academic motivation is positively correlated with school belonging, with a medium strength effect size (Allen et al., 2017). There has been some very interesting research conducted in this domain. For instance, using data from 90,118 adolescents across 132 secondary schools, Anderman (2002) found that a student's grade point average was positively related to school belonging. Goodenow and Grady (1993) found that academic motivation within a school context was positively associated with school belonging, but also much more influential than peer support or friendship groups. A study of 364 Turkish students found that students who feel valued and attached to their school environment are more likely to be academically motivated and succeed at school (Sari, 2012). In a study of 143 Mexican, Puerto Rican, and other Latino grade 12, academic motivation, measured in terms of engagement, academic aspirations and expectations, and grade point average, predicted school belonging (Sanchez, Colon, & Esparza, 2005). School belonging was also related to less absenteeism, which is consistent with past research that has also shown similar findings (e.g., Smerdon, 2002).

So academic motivation and school belonging are clearly related, but it's unclear which leads to the other. Indeed, there most likely is a reciprocal relationship. Like we saw with James, a sense of belonging can help students feel more motivated in their studies, while a sense of academic motivation can help students feel connected to the school that helps them meet a drive to learn. This means that developing a sense of belonging through the various strategies we've seen in the other modules might also help foster academic motivation. Alternatively, we can target academic motivation to help students feel a sense of belonging.

The studies that we reviewed used a variety of variables that broadly reflect aspects of academic motivation. Some of these were more closely related to school belonging than others, providing some hints as to what might help students be more academically motivated. Future aspirations and goals, academic self-regulation, self-academic rating, education goals, motivation, and valuing learning were more important than performance and achievement. That is, academic motivation does not necessarily need to be performance driven. It's about students who engage in positive academically motivated behaviours.

This is not to say academic outcomes are unimportant. We want our students to perform well academically. But how do we reach the desired outcomes? The past decade has demonstrated considerable pressure for students to achieve certain marks. Success is marked by grade point average, scores on standardised tests, and other objective outcomes. Yet at the same time, many students are disconnected with their learning or anxious about their performance. And in the process, the love of learning can be lost.

Our review suggest that it's the process of learning that matters more than specific outcomes. For instance, Stevens, Hamman, and Olivárez Jr (2007) explored the effect of teachers who used mastery goal orientation (learning new skills and mastering new situations, focused on the process of learning) versus a performance orientation (performance to perform well academically) with 434 early adolescents (average age 12.71 years). Students reported feeling greater belonging more when their teachers had a mastery goal orientation. Another study found that teachers who challenged their students, encouraged their ideas, and requested they explain their academic work (i.e., emphasising the learning process) fostered a greater sense of belonging – and better academic performance (Stevens et al., 2007).

In sum, a plethora of research has found that academic motivation not only is important for academic performance, but also is important for school belonging. And this research also suggests that school belonging is important for academic motivation. Wellbeing and academic success can go hand-in-hand when we focus on skills, attitudes, and behaviours that support the whole student (White & Kern, 2018). School leaders, staff, and teachers may benefit from implementing strategies for students that develop academic motivation, supporting both academic performance and school belonging.

Module overview

The activities in this module can be used with a group or class or adapted to work with an individual student. Rather than focusing on performance and achievement, the activities focus on the process of learning and development, targeting students' future aspirations, self-regulation, motivation, and learning to value school and learning.

Activity 1: The marshmallow challenge

Purpose: To increase connection and cooperation, and help students appreciate the value of prototyping and diverse skills.

Materials: For each group: 1 brown paper lunch bag, 20 sticks of spaghetti, 1 metre of string, 1-metre strip of masking tape, 1 marshmallow.

In addition; scissors, tape measure, upbeat music, countdown timer.

Suggested time for completion: 30–40 minutes.

Introduction

The marshmallow challenge teaches several important lessons on collaboration, innovation, and creativity, all in a fun and interactive manner. The activity itself takes 20 minutes to do, and it's important to end with the key lessons. For detailed instructions, including a TED talk by Tom Wujec, check out http://marshmallowchallenge.com.

Instructions

Before the session, prepare a set of materials for each group. For each group, you will need:

- 1 paper lunch bag (the brown ones work best, but you can use others if needed. The advantage of the brown bags is that it hides the materials until you start, adding an element of surprise. But the point of the bag is to keep the materials together, so even a clear plastic bag will work.
- 20 sticks of spaghetti (use regular spaghetti, not angel hair nor fettuccini)
- A piece of string, about 1 metre in length (a long arm's length)
- A piece of masking tape, about 1 metre in length (same length as the string – easier to stick these either to the tables or hang on a wall and allow students to collect for their group)
- 1 marshmallow (use regular sized, not the mini nor jumbo versions).

Also add a pair of scissors to each table or have a few pairs in the front of the room that students can use and have a tape measure on hand for measuring the height of the final structures. It's also useful to have some upbeat music to play in the background and put a countdown timer on the screen so students will know how much time they have remaining.

Have students get into teams of four to six and pass out the bags of materials. Tell them no peeking. Go through the instructions and answer any questions. Make sure all students are clear on the rules before beginning.

Instructions for students

When you open the bag, you'll find 20 sticks of spaghetti and a piece of string. There is a piece of tape for each group. And [take out a marshmallow], a nice light, fluffy marshmallow. When I tell you to begin, you will have 18 minutes to build the tallest free-standing structure only using the materials in the bag. The winning team is the one that can build the tallest free-standing structure with the marshmallow on top.

Now, there are some important rules that you must follow, or your team will be disqualified:

1   You will have 18 minutes, no more. When the music ends and I say stop, everyone must step away from the structure.

2   The structure must be built with the materials in the bag – the spaghetti, the string, the tape, and you can use the bag. You are welcome to cut or break these. However, the marshmallow must remain in one piece. No chewing it or breaking the marshmallow into pieces.

3   The marshmallow must be on top. I will measure from the base of the structure to the marshmallow. That means the structure cannot be hanging from a higher structure, such as a chair or bookshelf. You can build it either from the floor or the table, but not hanging off of any other furniture.

4   The structure must be freestanding. At the end of the 18 minutes, you will not be able to hold your structure up.

5   You can use as much or as little of the kit as you'd like. [Note: the official marshmallow challenge does not allow participants to use the bag. We have found that allowing this still keeps the task challenging, and students are even more creative.]

When students are clear on the instructions, let them begin. Start the countdown timer and play music to set a fun mood. Announce the time every so often (e.g., 10 minutes to go, 5 minutes to go, 3 minutes, 1 minute, countdown to the end). You can also challenge students further by commenting on the progress made by the different groups.

At the end of the 18 minutes, have the students stop and step away from the structure. Go around and measure the height, from the foundation to the marshmallow, then announce the winning team.

The task itself can be both frustrating and entertaining, helping to foster positive emotion and a sense of connection and friendly competition. But the real value comes from ending with a discussion about several key lessons that have been learned through the challenge. Bring the students back together to discuss these. We focus on two here [See the TED talk on the marshmallow challenge website (and the corresponding slides) for more details. We find it useful to go through the PDF to highlight the core lessons.]

- **Lesson 1: the value of prototyping – fail early and fail often**. We see that new business school graduates consistently perform poorly. In contrast, Prep and Year 1 students perform quite well. Why?

  The typical way that adults approach the task is to spend the first few minutes orienting themselves to the task (see what supplies are there, making sense of the task). They then spend some time planning and start building. They create a tall structure, carefully adding supports to the base. Then, in the last minute, they are ready for the "ta-da" moment, when they place the marshmallow on top. But often, the ta-da moment quickly becomes an "uh-oh" moment, as the weight of the marshmallow pulls the structure down.

  In contrast, young children will dive right into the task, creating a short structure with the marshmallow on top. Some will stand, some won't, but they play with it until it stands. But then they still have more time. So, they build more. This results in some fairly interesting structures, but the marshmallow ends up much higher – with no "uh-oh" moment.

We often spend a lot of time making grand plans and then when we are ready for the "ta-da" moment, we sometimes experience failure. Because we have invested so much time and effort into our plan, we don't always fix things. We can feel like a failure. Prototyping means that you try things out. Give it a go without much planning. Some things will work, others will fail – but you learn from mistakes, and keep iterating them into future successes.

• **Lesson 2: Diverse skills matter**. The marshmallow challenge highlights the value of diverse skills. When this task has been completed by business people, CEOs (the leaders of a company) tend to perform reasonably well on the task. But when the CEO is working with their administrative assistant, they do much better. Why? They have complementary skills. The CEO is good at thinking of big ideas, but the assistant is good at turning those ideas into reality. It's the combination of different skills that leads to the greatest success.

This ties in well with thinking about strengths. Each student has different strengths and things they are good at. Maybe one student has lots of great ideas. Another is good at following instructions. A third is good at calculating out what angle and level of support is needed for the weight of the marshmallow. It's by recognising and valuing different strengths and skills that we can, together, achieve the best.

Several other lessons can come from this task as well (see the marshmallow challenge website for more information). Also consider or ask the students what other lessons might be there, such as cooperation and creativity.

Activity 2: Valuing my school and classes

Purpose: To assist students to reflect on the value of school and education in relation to their personal goals.

Materials: *SWOT audit* worksheet (below and printable handouts available at https://www.routledge.com/9781138305083).

Suggested time for completion: 30–60 minutes, completed over 1 or 2 sessions.

Introduction

One of the challenges that schools face are the high number of disengaged students. Gallup (2014) found that only half of US students felt engaged in their learning, with a fifth actively disengaged, 10 per cent disengaged and discouraged with learning, and disengagement increasing across year levels. Similar reports have appeared in Australia and elsewhere around the world.

While it can be discouraging to see the statistics around student disengagement, there's also a hopeful story. Half of students *are* engaged in their learning. Many teachers are doing an amazing job connecting with their students, and many students really do care about their learning. And we can learn from their successes.

One way to help students connect more to school is to help them see the relevance of what they are learning. Often, negative student perceptions about school are not directed at classes, lessons, or even subjected material, rather it's at the lack of relevance of what they are being taught. It's hard to be excited about memorising facts for an exam, when you know that you'll never need to know that information again. Students may ask, what is the purpose of maths and literacy, when its only purpose is to score well on a standardised test?

But what if students understood that learning to write and read well could help them to communicate better with their beloved grandmother? Or that through maths class they could learn abstract ways to put ideas together, providing them with an important foundation to for becoming an engineer, designer, or businessperson? What if they understood that the "annoying" collaborative group project was actually teaching them the necessary social skills to become the next change-leader of the world? Students often fail to appreciate the value of school, but this issue can be easily addressed.

This activity helps students see the value – or the *perceived instrumentality* – in what they are doing at school. Studies find that perceived instrumentality has a positive impact on academic performance and motivation. This comes in part from passionate teachers who care about their students, are expert in their subject area, and are passionate about what they are teaching. But this also stems from a teacher's ability to help students connect their learning to their own interests and passions and help students learn to appreciate the opportunities for growth and development before them.

This activity involves three parts. First, students identify the benefits of school. The responses from the activity can provide good feedback to both teachers or practitioners around what students value most about their classes. It may also help students refocus or notice and appreciate what is being taught. Second, the activity guides students through a SWOT (strengths, weaknesses, opportunities, threats) evaluation to think deeper about their school experience. Third, students are asked to develop goals related to their discoveries.

The activity works well in a class or group, providing you with valuable feedback about the students' perceptions and experiences. It can also be used with an individual student, focusing on areas where they have more difficulties connecting.

Instructions

Part 1: Discovering the value of my classes

Break students into groups of three to five. First have the group identify things that they enjoy and see most valuable in the class. Have students note down their ideas on paper. Bring students back together and have some report back on what they came up with.

Invite students to return to their group, and now focus on a specific lesson. The aim is to glean why the lesson is important, whether or not you have made the relevance to their lives clear (often better if they are unclear on the relevance). For example, consider a lesson about Ancient Egypt. Something so removed from everyday life might seem boring and pointless. But learning about Ancient Egypt serves multiple functions, such as:

- determination and perseveration
- the benefits of achieving goals
- the importance of common goals and working together as a community
- the value of generational projects
- issues concerned with slavery and the importance of equality and human rights
- how early civilisations worked together
- the usefulness of writing and language to document findings and scientific advances in respect to astronomy, engineering, and mathematics so that it can be passed down through generations
- how the past will create a better future for ourselves by learning from the mistakes of others.

Select a lesson that has recently been taught in class, and have groups consider the deeper life lessons embedded in the lesson (you might have all groups focus on the same lesson, or have different groups focus on different lessons). Bring students back together and hear their ideas. Add any thoughts or insights that might have been missed.

Part 2: A SWOT analysis of my school

This next part expands the focus beyond a specific class to thinking about the school experience as a whole. Invite students to conduct a SWOT analysis of the school, individually or in groups, using the top section of the *SWOT audit* worksheet (below, printable handouts available at https://www.routledge. com/9781138305083). Give students 15–20 minutes to complete the analysis. If students get stuck, give ideas or invite questions to prompt their thinking.

Bring students back together. Work through each square, asking for some students to share the strengths, weaknesses, opportunities, and threats they see. Focus the conversation on the strengths and opportunities present, rather than the weaknesses and threats.

Part 3: Developing pathways forward from my discoveries

Hopefully the first two parts have revealed insights into what students value in class and at school, as well as identify opportunities, challenges, and threats inherent in the school environment. *Awareness* is a first step towards creating positive change. But it is important for students to translate new understandings into tangible actions. The final part of this activity asks students to create a goal from their SWOT analysis to help them connect better with a particular class or their school more generally.

Invite students to take a few minutes to complete the second part of the *SWOT analysis* worksheet, identifying one SMART goal related to class or school, based on their SWOT analysis, and several steps they can take to start pursuing that goal. If time allows, have students work in pairs to create an actionable plan for reaching their goals, otherwise give a few minutes for private reflection.

Bring students back together and have a few students share their goal and plans. Emphasise the importance of school and classes. You might like to reiterate that even if the value of a lesson is not always readily apparent, there are often deeper lessons present. A good challenge is to consider what *can* be taken away from the lesson.

A SWOT audit of my school

Part 1: The SWOT analysis

Different schools have different strengths and weaknesses. What is your school like? This activity asks you to audit or take stock of your school, by conducting a SWOT analysis. This is used a lot in business organisations to consider where they are doing well, where they can improve and what the best pathways are to achieve success. In the following four quadrants, indicate:

S: What are the *strengths* of your school?

W: What are the *weaknesses* of your school?

O: What are the *opportunities* within your school?

T: What are the *threats* that limit those opportunities?

Take a moment to reflect on these, then add your thoughts to each box. Be ready to share your thoughts with the class or the person who you are working with.

Strengths	Weaknesses
Opportunities	**Threats**

Part 2: Building on strengths

Take a moment to consider your analysis and the discussion that followed. Building on the strengths and opportunities of your school, what is one SMART goal related to a specific class or school more generally that you could take feel more connected to your learning?

What are some steps you can take to start pursuing this goal?

Additional thoughts and notes:

Activity 3: Finding my voice

Purpose: To help students feel empowered over their learning by contributing to class and reaching out to teachers for help when needed.

Materials: None.

Suggested time for completion: 30–40 minutes.

Introduction

As young people navigate the school environment and develop their own sense of identity, they want to feel valued. Their strengths and passions lie within, waiting for expression and development. Students with a sense of belonging feel that they can speak up and be included (Hensley, Place, Jordan, & Israel, 2007). Studies find that listening to students and encouraging their questions, perspectives, and insights help them connect with their learning (Hattie, 2004; Mitra, 2004; Smyth, 2006). Being able to speak candidly can foster relational trust (Fielding, 2004). If students and their teachers meet as 'equals' they will work as 'genuine partners' (Smyth, 2006). Rather than being taught materials, students become co-discoverers of information, with their teachers as their guides and supporters.

And yet many students feel stifled, whether by fear of criticism by peers, possible rejection by a teacher, self-doubt, or a variety of other factors. An important part of belonging is feeling safe and comfortable to voice your own thoughts and perspectives without criticism and rebuke. When a feeling of psychological safety is lacking, vulnerable students often respond by withdrawing or detaching. Some might become anxious over attending a class, while others might be fully present and perform well, but reframe from verbally contributing to discussions unless forced.

While teachers do their best to create a safe environment, students can also benefit from becoming comfortable in their own skin and feeling empowered to contribute. This activity aims to empower students to share their thoughts and feelings with their teachers, in class and beyond. Through role play, students identify blockers of speaking out and strategies around those perceived barriers. If working with an individual student, act as their partner to role play several scenarios.

Instructions

Begin by asking students to think about times in class where they felt uncomfortable contributing their thoughts and ideas. Or ask them to imagine feeling confused with a lesson – they consider asking the teacher for help, but don't. What stops them? After a moment of reflection, ask students to identify some of the things that stop them from speaking up. Basic reasons may include, "the teacher doesn't care" or "there are no opportunities", but try to encourage students to find deeper reasons such as, being afraid of what others might think.

Invite students to form groups of five to seven. Have one student sit in the middle of the group, with two students on either side – one as an encouraging voice, and the other as a negative voice. Others in the group will be observers and watch, contributing additional comments on the positive and/or negative side.

Ask students to act out a scenario where the student (person in the middle) wants to speak up in class but hesitates – one voice gives reasons why he or she should speak up, the other provides reasons not to. Encourage the observers to find ways to counter the negative voice. Switch roles for a new scenario where the student in the middle wants to seek help for an assignment or lesson after class. Switch roles and either repeat the scenarios several times or come up with other scenarios specific to the context in which you are working.

Bring the students back together. Ask students for some of the barriers they identified and how they worked through those. You may also like to ask what insights they discovered. Conclude by asking students to reflect on one or more of the following questions:

- Do you feel like you can talk to your teacher as an equal?
- What stops you from being able to talk to your teacher as an equal?
- What do you wish you could say to your classroom teacher to help your learning but haven't already?
- What is stopping you from talking to your teacher about your learning?
- How can you begin a conversation with your teacher?

Activity 4: Unearthing the roots of procrastination

Purpose: To help students overcome procrastination.

Materials: *Unearthing the roots of procrastination* worksheet (below and printable handouts available at https://www.routledge.com/9781138305083).

Suggested time for completion: 30–40 minutes.

Introduction

Do you ever have good intentions to do something, but keep putting it off? Even when we know that something is important, many other things grab our immediate attention. This can be especially true with tasks we don't particularly want to do – suddenly hanging out with friends, answering emails, cleaning the house, reordering your photos, and reading every story on social media seems so much more important and appealing. We can spend more time complaining or avoiding a task than the time it takes to actually do the task.

Procrastination is a common problem. Often it stems from trying to avoid something – consciously or subconsciously. While some tasks are boring, others stem from underlying fears and feelings of stress about our competence in completing the task. Procrastination becomes a way to avoid unpleasant feelings like frustration, stress, worry, and boredom.

As much as we may want to avoid some tasks, most of our necessary day-to-day undertakings (including exercise and homework assignments) are manageable for most people. Some tasks might be stressful momentarily, but when given time and effort, most people are able to complete them. And completing tasks (especially those we wanted to avoid) can give people a sense of satisfaction, positive emotions of relief, increased confidence, and even excitement.

This activity challenges students to unearth some of the root causes for procrastination, challenging them to replant those roots in healthier soil. It helps them identify strategies to embrace challenge head-on and reap the benefits.

Instructions

Begin by sharing with your students one of your own experiences with procrastination. What happened? What did you procrastinate about? How did it make you feel, especially as time became tight? What were the consequences?

Ask students to share tasks they procrastinate on. Then ask for some of the reasons why they do this. Try to unpack their responses. Are there common themes? Is the impending task stressful for them?

Discuss some of the consequences of procrastination – feelings of anxiety, worry, helplessness, and stress, loss of sleep, failing to complete other things on time. Especially consider the possible longer-term disadvantages of procrastinating. Perhaps it will affect the attainment of longer-term goals? Or long-term health outcomes?

Next, explain to students that one reason we procrastinate is to avoid negative feelings. A particular task we are trying to avoid might seem boring or we could feel anxious about being able to complete it. We might worry about our ability to finish it on time, and spend more time worrying about it than it actually takes to complete it. So we avoid these negative feelings with quick fixes that make us feel good in the moment (e.g., TV, social media, even cleaning!). Unfortunately, such habits create a negative cycle that increases the negative feelings that we were trying to avoid in the first place. The best thing we can do is sit with the discomfort momentarily, embrace the task, and reap the good feelings of successfully completing the task at hand.

Indicate to students that we often don't realise the reasons why we procrastinate – it just becomes habit. While completing the task as soon as possible is the obvious remedy to procrastination, that does not always happen and understanding why we procrastinate can help us develop useful strategies to overcome.

Note that we can think about procrastination like a plant that is growing in bad soil. At first it might do well – a plant grows and starts to flourish. But over time the bad soil will choke and destroy the plant. We might try to trim the plant down, add fertilizer, spray the growing weeds, or try other ways to help the plant, but all our efforts are in vain. What is needed is to change the soil that the plant is growing in. So we need to unearth the roots of the plant and replant it in a healthier place.

Similarly, with procrastination, it's helpful to unearth the reasons why we procrastinate, and then identify healthier strategies – like moving the plant to healthier soils.

Invite students to complete the *Unearthing the roots of procrastination* work-sheet (below; printable handouts available at https://www.routledge.com/9781138305083) individually or in pairs. If working in pairs, have the partners challenge each other to fully unearth deeper reasons for procrastination and generate alternative solutions.

Bring students back together and discuss insights that came up. Challenge them to try and apply their strategy over the next week, emphasising that possibly the fastest solution to avoiding procrastination is to do the task straight away.

Unearthing the roots of procrastination

We often procrastinate on tasks that we need to do to avoid negative feelings, such as boredom, anxiety, and worry. So, we do other things that make us feel good. But the task does not go away on its own and can create growing amounts of stress and worry about getting it done.

Procrastination is like a plant growing up in bad soil. The plant tries to grow strong but becomes more and more unhealthy as the soil drains its life away. What is needed is to dig up the plant at its roots and replant it into healthy soil. While confronting such tasks can create negative feelings, these are temporary feelings, and if you tackle a task straight away and stick with it, you'll feel a lot better when it's done.

Take a few minutes and consider the following questions to help unearth the reasons why you procrastinate and think of ways to identify healthy ways to embrace challenge.

What tasks you procrastinate on? Note a few tasks here.

What are the short- and long-term consequences of procrastinating?

What would you gain from not procrastinating?

Now let's unearth the reasons why you procrastinate. Focus on one of the tasks listed above. List all the reasons you can think of as to why you procrastinate.

What could you do to avoid procrastinating? Create a game plan to confront the task head-on. Identify specific steps to take.

Activity 5: Rocks of life

Purpose: To help students develop a study routine.

Materials: *Rocks of Life* worksheet (below and printable handouts available at https://www.routledge.com/9781138305083), two large clear jars, rocks of a range of sizes (enough to overflow the jars), sand, water.

Suggested time for completion: 20–30 minutes.

Introduction

Ever wonder where your time goes? One of the most common complaints people have is that they don't have enough time to do what they want or need to do. While we can have periods where everything seems to happen at once, often it's more our perception of, and use of time, that makes us feel that way. The truth is, we usually have time for the things that we make time for. Some of the most successful individuals are very busy – but manage to fit in going to the gym or having dinner each night with their family. Why is that? They purposely schedule the things that matter, and the less important things must fit around those priorities. Often we fill our time with things that matter less, making it difficult to find time for the things we care about.

This activity visually helps students think about how they spend their time, and then challenges them to purposefully schedule time for their studies. It takes a bit of time and effort to set up, in terms of gathering sand, rocks, water and jars. It's also useful to trial this a few times to determine the right proportions of rocks, sand, and water.

As students complete the worksheet, some students might struggle with identifying which are higher versus lower priority activities/ tasks; it is useful to watch out for this and provide guidance (encouraging them to focus on school-related tasks, but also being open to their perspective on what should be a priority). It is also helpful to do this in combination with Activity 6 in this module, which focuses on motivation for making studying a priority.

Instructions

Begin by asking students to share some of the ways that they spend their time. Ask where studying fits into these activities. Note that studying is an important part of being a successful student. But it can be hard to find time for studying amidst all the other things you can be doing, such as hanging out with friends, playing online games, or staying on top of your social media feeds. You might find yourself trying to complete assignments or study for an exam at the last minute because you ran out of time.

Place one of the clear jars on the table. Fill it part way with sand. Note that the sand is like all the little things that take our attention. They aren't particularly important, but add up, and take a lot of our time. Then add small rocks.

These rocks are more important things. Add some bigger rocks. Then try to put the largest rocks inside (they should not be able to fit inside with the sand and smaller rocks inside). These large rocks are the really important things – those that we either really care about or know that we need to care about, such as our studies. What happens when we try to add them to the jar? There's not enough room.

Take the second jar. Place the bigger rocks inside. What happens if we put the big rocks in first? They fit well. Add smaller rocks, then the sand. Note that little rocks fit around the big rocks, and the sand fills in around the rocks. Then add water. We find we even have space for a bit of extra – represented by the water. By placing the big rocks in first, we make sure they fit, and other things fit around them.

Note that our time is a lot like this. We often fill it with lots of little things that don't matter. So, when we go to do what's important – our big rocks, we don't have time, because we're all filled up with the little things. By adding our big rocks first – what matters most to us or the tasks that we need to do to be successful as a student – we find that we do actually have more time than we first thought.

Next, hand out the *Study rocks* worksheet (see page 135; printable hand-outs available at https://www.routledge.com/9781138305083). Explain that a helpful way to prioritise your time (and drawing from the metaphor, "make sure you put your big rocks in first") is to create a study timetable. Invite students to first list their upcoming study tasks (assignments, exams, readings, et cetera.), along with other priorities that they have (e.g., spending time with friends, taking care of siblings) and activities they are involved in (e.g., sports teams, clubs, et cetera.). Number the tasks in terms of importance (1 being the most important). Then, fill in the timetable, placing the most important tasks first, and then filling in the other tasks, activities, and events.

Give students a bit of time to work, individually or in pairs or small groups. Most likely they will not finish but encourage them to make a good start on it. Then bring them back together for final thoughts and reflections. Note some of the following tips that can be helpful:

1   Don't just plot the due dates, schedule when you will actually work on the task that is due.
2   Due dates don't have to be the date you submit your work. You can actually submit work earlier!
3   Work on tasks and assignments early so it affords you time to ask questions and get help if needed.
4   Set false due dates a week or so before the assignment is due to give you some time to buffer unexpected events or circumstances that might crop up.
5   List specific tasks that you will do rather than broad descriptions of activities. For example, don't say, "Essay" – be specific like, "Research and write introduction to essay". This will help you break the task down into steps and allow you a sufficient amount of time to complete each task.

Encourage students to fill their timetable out further over the next few days and aim to revise it each week. Note that it can be particularly beneficial to start each week mapping out tasks, taking stock of upcoming activities, commitments, and what needs to be done, and making sure to place the big rocks in first and filling in the other bits around those big rocks. Also note that creating such a timetable can be challenging at first, but gets easier with practice – so be willing to give it a go for a few weeks and see if it is useful.

Rocks of life

Take a few minutes and list all of the activities, obligations, tasks, and things you'd like to be able to do over the next week. Be as specific as possible. Include both school-related and non-school related activities. List both big and small things, noting any due dates for assignments or exams. Then, number each task in terms of its importance (1 = essential, 2 = quite important, 3 = moderately important, 4 = a little important, 5 = unimportant).

Task/ Activity	Importance

Now fill out the table below, indicating when you will do each activity/ task, starting with the most important tasks (your big rocks, labelled 1), and proceeding to the least important (the sand and water).

Monday	Tuesday	Wednesday	Thursday	Friday	Saturday	Sunday

Activity 6: Fruits of success

Purpose: To help motivate students towards developing discipline and study routines.

Materials: None.

Suggested time for completion: 30 minutes.

Introduction

Motivation to learn plays an important role in being successful at school. Research shows that motivated students study harder, perform better, engage more, and feel a greater sense of belonging than unmotivated students.

One of the major theories in psychology, Self-Determination Theory (SDT; Deci & Ryan, 2008), suggests that there are different types of motivation, which range on a spectrum from being very internally motivated (*intrinsic motivation* – you do things because you want to do them, simply for the joy of the activity itself) to being not motivated at all (*amotivation*). In between the two types of motivation are a variety of externally motivated reasons for engaging in an activity (*extrinsic motivation*), such as to obtain a reward, or because doing the task will help you achieve another goal that you care about (e.g., by doing well on this exam, it will help me become a doctor).

Some students are driven by a strong desire for success or may have a continued curiosity of learning – they are intrinsically motivated. Others are driven by their parents or others, so they work hard to make others happy – a form of extrinsic motivation. And other students are amotivated – they really could not care less about their academic performance and ability to learning. Such students can get stuck in a rut of inactivity as they wait for motivation to come.

The reality is that many young people will never FEEL like doing homework. It will never become an intrinsic love. But there are a variety of externally motivated approaches that can be used to help students get things done.

One such strategy is to make studying a discipline – whether you want to do it or not. Often, the hardest part is getting started. With no motivation to study, other things seem more interesting and important to do. But once you get started, it's easier to keep going. Some of the highest achievers have struggled a lot with motivation, but they keep moving forward anyway – out of habit, they dive into the tasks needed, even if they don't want to.

For instance, athletes engage in considerable repetitive training. There can be many days when the swimmer has no desire to watch the black line pass under them over and over again, the runner would rather stay in bed than go for a run in the rain and cold, the weight lifter would rather not pick up another piece of iron. But they do it anyway. Out of habit, the goggles come on, the shoes are laced up, the weight is lifted. Similarly, some of the most successful writers and artists have a strict routine. For instance, Graham Greene famously wrote 1000 words a day. Each day a writer or artist might sit down to write or create, and follow the same routine, whether or not words come. Through habit, inspiration eventually comes. Self-discipline and routine may be more important than motivation.

Likewise, students can benefit from making studying a routine – making it a habit, something they simply do, whether or not they feel like doing it. One technique that has been used effectively in writing – and can be applied to homework tasks – is the *Pomodoro Technique*, developed by Italian Francesco Cirillo (2006). The idea is to sit down for a limited period of time, indicated by a timer. You work until the timer sounds – and then earn a Pomodoro! Take a short rest, then repeat, sometimes with longer rest intervals, sometimes with shorter intervals.

This activity introduces students to the Pomodoro Technique, using several short intervals. The idea is to teach them the technique, then challenge them to incorporate it into their studies. Have fun with this! Some ideas to get you started:

- It can be helpful to start with shorter intervals, and then work to extend those over time.
- Mix up intervals, with some longer periods, some shorter periods, and varying the amount of rest. Mix it up across different days, or the amount of time spent on various tasks.
- Have the students create a training schedule, intermixing longer and shorter study periods.
- The original is a Pomodoro (*tomato* in Italian), but use other fruits (or have students choose their favourite fruit).
- Have a fruit competition. See how many fruits students can earn over the week (with prizes for the most fruit, but also the most creative mix or other variants)
- There are various mobile phone apps to help with this technique, helping to set intervals and manage time.

Instructions

Begin with a discussion around some of the challenges that students find in making time to study and do their assignments. Invite them to consider the role that motivation plays. Ask what happens when they don't feel motivated to do things. Do they do it anyway, or set it aside? Note that this is an activity to help them get things done, even when they don't feel like it.

Next, introduce the Pomodoro technique. With the group, practise with short segments, but the idea is for students to extend their Pomodoros into longer sessions. The ideal time is between 20 and 35 minutes per session (Cirillo, 2006).

Set a timer for 5 minutes. Have the students engage in a non-interrupted study task (e.g., writing, note-taking, reading). Students must work until the timer rings.

Take a 1-minute break. Congratulate the students, noting they've earned their first Pomodoro (or other fruit). Give students a 1-minute rest and reset the timer. Again, have students work for 5 minutes. Repeat (1-minute rest, 5 minutes work).

Bring the students back together and congratulate them on earning 3 Pomodoros. Explain the process and set up the challenge for them to trial this technique over the next week, increasing their time to 20 to 35 minutes.

Activity 7: The wall of failure

Purpose: To help students recognise mistakes and failures as learning opportunities.

Materials: None.

Suggested time for completion: 20–30 minutes.

Introduction

We all make mistakes despite our best efforts and these experiences can result in negative or unpleasant feelings. Mistakes and failure are a part of the rich tapestry of life, and yet as a culture, we tend to be fairly averse to failure, and so we avoid failure at all costs. While this has the benefits of not experiencing the negative feelings of failure, or even the social judgment of messing things up, it can limit our experiences and our potential for success. If we can embrace failure and re-frame mistakes into opportunities, mistakes and failures can become important opportunities for growth and learning.

In a famous example, the undomesticated habits of scientist Sir Alexander Fleming were clear when he returned home from a two-week holiday. He left dirty dishes in the sink when he departed, and returned to find bacteria growing on the dishes. He could have responded with horror or disgust and dumped the contents into the rubbish. But instead, Sir Alexander was intrigued by the growth, and upon careful investigation, it was the roots of his ground-breaking discovery of penicillin.

Within the school context, Professor Andrew Martin (2017) from the University of Western Sydney, among many others, has written extensively about the importance of academic resilience. In this space, there is a growing understanding that failure is fundamentally important for learning. While not all of our mistakes will be revolutionary, we can grow to understand that it's not so much whether or not mistakes happen and failures occur, but how we respond that matters. Do we give up or do we learn, refine, and move forward?

This activity aims to help students embrace mistakes and failure, identifying ways to reframe them into learning opportunities, rather than as reasons for defeat.

Instructions

Begin by asking students to think about some of the mistakes or failures they've made. Give a personal story of a mistake that you made, especially if things turned out well in the end. For instance, Kelly once made the mistake of applying for a job in genetics research. The job interview was a massive failure, but it prompted her to turn to studying psychology instead, which led her to doing her PhD with Professors Lea Waters and Dianne Vella-Brodrick, meeting Peggy Kern and writing this book!

Next, read the following script:

> It's easy to get bogged down by mistakes or failures we make, and we can spend too much time thinking about them in unproductive ways. We might blame ourselves or others for our mistakes. We might become distressed or upset by them. So perhaps we try to avoid doing things that will cause us to fail in the future. That can help us feel better, as we only do the things that we know we can do successfully.
>
> But if we can look at mistakes or failures as learning opportunities, they can actually help us learn and grow. This means shifting the way that we think about mistakes and failures – turning them into opportunities.
>
> Professor Martin from the University of Western Sydney knows a lot about learning and talks frequently about failure in his lectures. He uses a metaphor of building a wall to describe a productive way of managing a mistake and we are going to try that out today.
>
> Close your eyes. In your mind recall a mistake you have recently made. It might be something really big, or just a small mistake. Next, mentally build a wall around your mistake. Visually build it in your mind out of whatever materials you choose.
>
> Now consider trying to go through the wall. You walk up to it, but it pushes you back. You can't get around it – you are stuck – it's stopping you from moving forward. You are trapped by your mistake, and you must sit with the discomfort.
>
> After acknowledging the discomfort, you need to decide, are you going to let the wall stop you from moving on, leaving you to wallow in your mistake for ever? Or are you going to conquer your mistake, take away a lesson or two, then move on and climb over the wall?
>
> Next, visualise climbing up and over the wall. It's challenging, but you are able to put one foot in front of the over and accomplish the task of reaching the other side. As you reach the top of the wall you stop to look out at the view. You see the big picture, which helps you put things into perspective. And perhaps your mistake looks rather small in comparison. And as you land on the other side of the wall, imagine feeling a sense of accomplishment and freedom. You are no longer trapped by your mistake, but are free to move on, with renewed vigour and knowledge.

Building a wall around the mistake allows you to acknowledge the mistake, rather than ignoring it. It helps you take ownership of your part in the mistake, and learn how to do things differently in the future. Climbing over the wall helps you to move forward and grow stronger, even learning from the experience.

Next, have students think about a major task or event that occurred, where they felt they really stuffed things up or felt like a failure. Something where they felt really awful. Then, have students pair up with a partner (if working with an individual student, act as their partner). One will act as the coach, the other the coachee. The coach should guide the coachee through the following questions:

1   Building the wall: First, tell me about a time that you felt like you really stuffed things up. Describe what happened What were you thinking at the time? How did it make you feel?
2   Climbing the wall: Looking back at it now, what are one or two things you took away from that event?
3   Moving beyond the wall: What could you do differently the next time around in a similar situation? What did you learn that can help you in the future?

Have students switch roles and repeat. Finally, bring them back together for final discussion and reflection. Remind them that mistakes, failures, and knockbacks can be a gift. They can leave space for new opportunities. Sometimes we can certainly be better off for having made them. Encourage students to consider the wall the next time they make a mistake or feel like a failure. Visualise your mistake, build a wall around it, face the mistake. Then visualise climbing over the wall, gaining perspective and a sense of empowerment as you move beyond the wall with your new-found knowledge that you did not have before.

Activity 8: Springboards and sinkholes

Purpose: To help students identify barriers and enablers to learning.

Materials: *Springboards and sinkholes* worksheet (printable handouts available at https://www.routledge.com/9781138305083).

Suggested time for completion: 20–30 minutes.

Introduction

Whenever we complete a task, some things help (enablers) whereas other things get in our way (barriers). Some of these enables or barriers are internal (e.g., our mindset, level of self-confidence, personality, motivation), whereas others are external (e.g., demands from friends or family, competing activities, the environment we are functioning in). The internal and external enables and barriers interact with one another, impact on our thoughts, emotions, and behaviours. For instance, you might be really motivated to complete a task, but then there are a lot of demands on your time and energy from work and family. Over time, you lose motivation for the task, and it never gets done.

The same is true for learning. Students don't disconnect from learning immediately – it's a slow slide that happens as a growing number of internal and external barriers get in the way. In contrast, enablers can help us be successful, even when barriers are present. For instance, a student might really struggle understanding algebra, and has little desire to study. But their parents really encourage them, a teacher connects with them after each class to help them with their studies, and they have a good friend who offers to do homework together. The student successfully completes the assignments and excels in the class.

Often, we don't recognise the enablers and disablers that are in and around us. Our attention can become increasingly focused on the barriers, such that we lose sight of, or take for granted, the enablers. This activity helps students take stock of their barriers and enablers, challenging them to seek out the enablers (springboards propelling them on their school journey) and escape the barriers (sinkholes that can stop them).

Instructions

Begin with the following script:

> Imagine that you are part of a video game. Your goal is to traverse the countryside to Mt Fujimato to recover the golden treasure that was stolen from your village. As you head out on your journey, you encounter all sorts of challenges – villains who try to beat you up, peaks you have to climb over, and sinkholes – big pits that trap you and won't let you escape, unless someone else comes along and rescues you. But there are also things that help you. You can find coins along the way, which give you extra strength, powers to defeat certain villains, and springboards that let you fly over valleys and mountains, speeding along your journey.
>
> Your journey through school can be like that video game. There are lots of barriers that stop you, making you feel disconnected from learning and school. Like sinkholes, you can feel stuck, and wonder why you have to suffer through your classes and the work they entail. Then there are the springboards – people and resources that help motivate you and keep you going along your journey.
>
> Some of these sinkholes and springboards are inside of us – like our thoughts, our personality, and our emotions – and others are things around us – like our friends, activities that we do, and technology.

Invite students to brainstorm some internal and external enablers (springboards) and barriers (sinkholes). Then, hand out the *Springboards and sinkholes* work-sheet (see below; printable handouts available at https://www.routledge. com/9781138305083). Working in groups of three to five, have students iden-tify sinkholes that stop them from connecting with school and learning and springboards that help them feel more motivated and able to be successful at school. As students work, provide additional ideas when they get stuck, chal-lenging them to be creative.

Bring the students back together for further reflection and wrap up. Note that sinkholes can seem really big. Sometimes we can feel stuck, like there is no way to get out. Sometimes we do not even realise that we are stuck in the sinkhole, but we struggle along, feeling more and more stuck. It's helpful to recognise the sinkholes – then we can start doing something about them. Turning our focus on our springboards can help us escape the sinkholes and propel ourselves and each other forward to be successful students.

Springboards and sinkholes

Consider your journey through school. There can be heaps of sinkholes along the way – things that get in the way of your learning, making it hard to connect to school. Then there are springboards – things that propel you forward, motivating you to study hard, connect with your classmate, and succeed at the tasks needed. Take stock of your sinkholes and springboards. Be creative – think of both internal and external things, big and small.

Springboards (enablers) to my learning

Sinkholes (blockers) to my learning

Module wrap up: Suggested questions for personal reflection or discussion

1 What do you understand about mistakes since completing this module?
2 How would you advise a friend if they were having trouble with procrastination?
3 Why is it better not to wait around until you feel "motivated" to do homework?

Final thoughts

This module has provided various activities to help empower students to take control of their learning journey, identify the value of school, develop strategies to overcome procrastination, structure study time, and build motivation. We identified enablers and barriers of learning, and considered how failures and mistakes can be incorporated into the learning journey.

While these strategies can help some students become more engaged in their learning, other students have very real barriers to learning. They may be students with learning difficulties, mental illness, behavioural issues, trauma backgrounds et cetera. Such issues can seriously impede motivation to learn and connect with school. It is important for school staff to work with parents and external professionals to identify the barriers to learning that a young person may face. The conclusion may result in referral to learning support services, additional intervention, or additional testing. Strategies and support may be implemented. We believe that all students can still benefit from the activities in this module, but for some students, the activities may require some additional scaffolding and discretion in how the activities are applied.

It is important that school level strategies also be considered for a student who is disconnected from learning or exhibiting signs of school refusal. Involvement at the school level is crucial. Teachers or Year level coordinators need to be informed, as there are practical school accommodations that can be made (e.g., modified timetable, seating arrangements, reduction of stressors, differentiation of work tasks, additional programming, external support, et cetera).

At times, as problems continue for a young person, they might request to change classes or schools. While this may indicate a problem, changing schools is not necessarily the best solution and such a decision should not be made lightly. In the first instance, where safe and appropriate to do so, finding ways to address the student's or parent's concerns is a good starting place. This may require one-on-one or group-based work, support group meetings to find out further information and consultation with school leaders. It can be useful for parents, school leaders, staff, and the young person to consider:

- Are school staff hearing the concerns of the child?
- Are school staff acting on the concerns of the child?

- What interventions and strategies have the school put in place to address these concerns?
- How has the school helped or empowered the child to overcome their concerns?
- Are school staff communicating with parents effectively?
- Are parents communicating with the school effectively?
- How can communication and alliance between school and parents be strengthened?
- Is the student in imminent risk?

Students should be asked for the reasons why they want to change schools, considering the sources of discontent.

Of course, the decision to change schools can be the best outcome for a student, especially if there are issues concerned with bullying, victimisation, ostracization, isolation, a toxic school culture, or inadequate support for the student's needs. We just ask that school leaders, teachers, and practitioners prompt parents to consider school changes carefully. Changing schools outside of regular transition points, can create a decline in school belonging as students need to draw on personal resources to find ways to re-connect with a new setting (e.g., new teachers, new peers, new resources, et cetera). And this can take time.

References

Allen, K., Kern, P. Vella-Brodrick, D., & Waters, L. (2017) School values: A comparison of academic motivation, mental health promotion, and school belonging with student achievement. *Educational and Developmental Psychologist, 34*(1), 31–47.

Anderman, E. M. (2002). School effects on psychological outcomes during adolescence. *Journal of Educational Psychology, 94*(4), 795–809.

Cirillo, F., (2006). The Pomodoro technique. Retrieved from https://francescocirillo. com/pages/pomodoro-technique

Deci, E. L., & Ryan, R. M. (2008). Self-determination theory: A macrotheory of human motivation, development, and health. *Canadian Psychology, 49*, 182–185.

Fielding, M. (2004). New wave student voice and the renewal of civic society. *London Review of Education, 2*(3), 197–217.

Gallup. (2014). *Gallup student poll technical report.* Retrieved from www.gallup.com/ topic/gallup_student_poll.aspx

Goodenow, C., & Grady, K. E. (1993). The relationship of school belonging and friends' values to academic motivation among urban adolescent students. *Journal of Experimental Education, 62*(1), 60–71.

Hattie, J. (2004). It's official: Teachers make a difference. *Educare News: The National Newspaper for All Non-government Schools, 144*, 24–31.

Hensley, S. T., Place, N. T., Jordan, J. C., & Israel, G. D. (2007). Quality 4-H youth development program: Belonging. *Journal of Extension, 45*(5), Article 5FEA8. Retrieved from http://www.joe.org/joe/2007october/a8.shtml

Libbey, H. P. (2004). Measuring student relationships to school: Attachment, bonding, connectedness, and engagement. *Journal of School Health, 74*(7), 275–283.

Martin, A. J. (2017). *Motivating and engaging the 21st century learner: Critical principles and processes for success.* Keynote Presentation at New South Wales Deputy Principals Association State Conference, Hyatt Regency, Sydney, Australia.

Mitra, D. L. (2004). The significance of students: Can increasing "student voice" in schools lead to gains in youth development? *Teachers College Record, 106*(4), 651–688.

Ryan, R. M., & Deci, E. L. (2000). Self-determination theory and the facilitation of intrinsic motivation, social development, and wellbeing. *American Psychologist, 55,* 68–78.

Sanchez, B., Colon, Y., & Esparza, P. (2005). The role of sense of school belonging and gender in the academic adjustment of Latino adolescents. *Journal of Youth and Adolescence, 34*(6), 619–628.

Sari, M. (2012). Sense of school belonging among elementary school students. *Çukurova University Faculty of Education Journal, 41*(1), 1–11.

Smerdon, B. A. (2002). Students' perceptions of membership in their high schools. *Sociology of Education, 75*(4), 287–305.

Smyth, J. (2006). When students have power: Student engagement, student voice, and the possibilities for school reform around 'dropping out' of school. *International Journal of Leadership in Education: Theory and Practice, 9*(4), 285–298.

Stevens, T., Hamman, D., & Olivárez Jr., A. (2007). Hispanic students' perception of white teachers' mastery goal orientation influences sense of school belonging. *Journal of Latinos and Education, 6*(1), 55–70. doi: 10.1080/15348430709336677

White, M. A., & Kern, M. L., (2018). Positive education: Learning and teaching for wellbeing and academic mastery. *International Journal of Wellbeing, 8*(1), 1–17. doi: 10.5502/ijw.v8i1.588.

6 Connecting with help

The first time I saw [the school psychologist] I was scared, but when I realised that she was just like talking to any other adult, I felt comfortable.

~ *Joanne, age 17*

Module at a glance

In brief

This module explores the relationship between mental health and school belonging. It aims to help students understand themselves and identify relevant support resources.

Learning outcomes

- Assess stress level and mental health.
- Identify and evaluate different coping strategies.
- List their own personal help seeking resources.

Contents

A case study: A friend in need

There was a hive of bustle and emotion outside the school psychologist's office one morning. A group of Year 7 girls stood outside, teetering about whether or not they should knock. Samantha took the lead and gave a timid knock, and the four friends were soon nervously sitting in the counselling room. The psychologist began by carefully explaining the limits of confidentiality. While this is a common conversation with any client, it seemed especially important with this group, as the psychologist had a hunch they wanted to disclose something that could have safety or legal considerations for another student or teacher.

Samantha timidly voiced their communal concern. They were increasingly worried about their friend Charlise. They had noticed that at times there were cuts on her arms, and lately she was acting rather distant from them. When asked if she was OK, she would brush off their concerns, or snappishly note that she was fine. The girls cared about Charlise, but were both worried about her and rather annoyed with her behaviour. So they had made their way to the school psychologist to seek advice.

The school psychologist first praised the girls for speaking with an adult about a topic that was very sensitive. They needed reassurance that they had done the right thing. At this point they were worried that they were tattling on Charlise and that Charlise may now find herself in trouble. The school psychologist discussed that it was important for Charlise to see her so that she could ensure that she is safe. At first, they were mortified that the school psychologist would speak to Charlise, but once the school psychologist explained that keeping secrets and not acting on their concerns could result in far worse outcomes than Charlise feeling upset, they could see that it made sense. After all, they came to the school psychologist in the first place to ensure that Charlise was OK.

Charlise was invited to see the school psychologist during the following break. The school psychologist carefully explained that some information had been shared and that others in the school were concerned about her, so this was just an opportunity for her to check in and see if she could use any extra support. The school psychologist protected the anonymity of Samantha and the other girls, as that may have created conflict with Charlise, leading to the loss of an important social support network.

Charlise was angry at first, but as rapport was developed, Charlise broke down, revealing that she was experiencing conflict at home with her mother and father. She felt like she was always in trouble and that her A+ student brother, who saves money and keeps his bedroom impeccably clean, is the golden child of the family. She felt immensely pressured to be successful in her classes, but struggled to understand the material. She never felt like she was good enough for her father, no matter what she did or how hard she tried. About a month ago, she had seen a character on television purposely cut themselves to relieve pain. She was intrigued with the idea and tried it, just small cuts that brought a bit of blood – no big deal. While it hurt at first, she suggested that the physical pain took away some of the emotional pain – cutting became a way of dealing with the stress in her life. Over the past month, the cuts became a bit bigger and more visible, leading to the concerns that brought her friends to the psychologist's office.

On questioning, there was no suicidal intent to her actions and she appeared to have used cutting as a maladaptive coping strategy. Charlise provided consent to contact her parents, and over multiple sessions, the psychologist worked with Charlise, both to identify the sources of stress and to develop positive coping strategies. Fortunately, thanks to her friends, intervention was able to happen early, before cutting became habitual and highly self-destructive.

What the research says

The psychological and emotional wellbeing of students has become an increasing priority, especially in light of the growing incidence of depression, suicide, and anxiety amongst students that has occurred over the past few decades (Allen & McKenzie, 2015), combined with increasingly earlier ages of onset (Kessler & Bromet, 2013).

Notably, mental health and school belonging often go hand-in-hand. Students struggling with mental health issues often struggle in their relationships, which in turn can contribute further to mental illness. Indeed, numerous studies find that poor mental health is negatively associated with a sense of belonging (Allen et al., 2018; McMahon, Parnes, Keys, & Viola, 2008; Shochet et al., 2007). For instance, Anderman (2002) found that students' higher individual levels of school belonging were related to lower levels of depression, a finding also supported by Shochet et al. (2006) and Kia-Keating and Ellis (2007). McMahon et al. (2008) suggested that students face social stressors at schools (e.g., peer rejection, peer victimisation, and peer harassment), which correlate with psychological problems. McMahon et al. further suggested that environmental structures within schools, such as safety, discipline, and fairness need to be considered.

Long before a student presents in the psychologist's office with a diagnosis of a mental health disorder, students often find various ways to try to cope with negative feelings. Self-harm, like we saw in the case of Charlise, is not uncommon in secondary schools. Many teenagers that engage in self-harm have no suicidal intent; rather it is a way to deal with the emotions and struggles they face. Young people are navigating a time in their life that can be unpredictable, turbulent and personally challenging. They need to learn be able to identify and use positive coping strategies.

But young people often are unsure of how to cope effectively with day-to-day stressors. They can be influenced by the media, online posts, peers, and other sources that provide unhelpful, maladaptive, or even harmful solutions, including alcohol and drug use, avoidance, self-harm, disordered eating or sleeping patterns, risky behaviours, or excessive gaming. While some experimentation may do little harm, many of these maladaptive coping methods become increasingly harmful and harder to change as they become more habitual and in-grained, in many cases even altering the young person at a neurological level. What begins as an inability to cope can spiral into a myriad of mental health disorders or worse.

Schools need to make sure that pathways for help are known by students. Do students know when and how to seek help? Does the school psychologist (or other support personal e.g., counsellor, nurse, chaplain) have a presence in the school? Do most students know who they can access support from? Like we saw with Charlise, early intervention with the psychologist was able to shift maladaptive patterns before they became too ingrained.

Teachers also can play an important role in providing a first line of support and encouragement, teaching and modelling positive coping strategies, and recognising early signs of mental health problems. Schools can benefit from providing professional development for teachers around mental health, and developing clear policy and practices around referral procedures and support seeking.

Further, young people often first turn to their mates for help (White & Kern, 2018). Teaching students how to help friends provides a mutual form of support. And finally, there are strategies that a young person can implement to proactively care for their own mental health, getting support as needed.

With mental health, a preventative approach is clearly beneficial – the more that students can identify and develop adaptive strategies for coping with challenges *before* troubles occur, the better off they will be *when* challenges come along. This includes understanding and being able to draw on internal and external resources available, as well as being able and willing to seek help from others – including peers, parents, teachers, and professionals – when needed.

Module overview

The module aims to help students develop skills and confidence for coping with challenges, seek help when needed, and to feel empowered to help others. The activities come from a proactive framework, helping to prevent bigger mental health problems from occurring. However, if any student presents with suicide ideation, depression, anxiety, or other major mental health concerns, it's important to take appropriate steps to refer them to therapy or other forms of professional support. The activities can be done with individuals or groups. With a group or class, be mindful to ensure the information offered by young people is kept safe and confidential. Students should be aware of the disadvantages of public disclosure and that should they wish to disclose something personal that there are other spaces that are also appropriate (e.g., with the school psychologist).

Activity 1: Stress perceptions

Purpose: To help students better understand stress and start to consider effective stress management strategies.

Materials: None.

Suggested time for completion: 15–20 minutes.

Introduction

"Stress" is a word that has become a common part of our modern-day parlance – especially for students. They are stressed over exams, assignments, presentations, social interactions, trying to keep up with social media feeds . . . the list goes on and on. Stress is seen as a bad thing. Professor Daniel Keating (2017) from the University of Michigan wrote "There are new clues that the high levels of stress many people endure every day are taking a deadly toll" (para. 1). We have become a fast-paced society, with unevenly distributed power structures, and high pressure to achieve at all costs. In Australia, Year 11 and 12 students are the most stressed compared with any other year level at school.

Stress indeed can have negative effects, physically and psychologically. Our systems are well-tuned to recognise threat, which can trigger a "fight-or-flight" response (Cannon, 1932). According to this classical model, when a stressor is perceived, your physiological system is stimulated into a heightened state – your heart beat speeds up, eyes dilate, breathing speeds up, hunger decreases, cortisol increases, and immune function goes down, as your system is ready to either fight against the threat or run away (flight). After the stressor passes, the parasympathetic system kicks in to calm you down, slowing the heart, slowing your breath, reducing cortisol, and bringing things back to normal.

The fight-or-flight response is certainly adaptive if you come across a poisonous snake in the bush, your child runs toward the street, or you are running to catch a flight. But it also uses a lot of energy. It's an acute response to a limited stressor. But problems can arise when that stress becomes more chronic. If your system is constantly stimulated, without recovery, it places pressure on your physiological system. Indeed, we do see that chronic stress increases risk for heart disease, immune disorders, and other physical illnesses. We also see that chronic stress affects cognitive and psychological functioning (Friedman & Kern, 2012; Kemeny, 2007; McEwen, 2006; Segerstrom & Miller, 2004).

However, it's also important to distinguish between *stressors* and *stress*. Stressors are external or internal challenges against our physiological or psychological system. *Stress* involves both the stressor itself and your *perception* of the stressor. Stress is a normal part of life – and can be good (eustress) or bad (distress). The effect that is has on our physiological system depends on our perception – conscious or subconscious – about our ability to cope. Eustress occurs when we believe we have adequate resources, or we see the stressor as desirable, whereas distress occurs when we feel unable to cope. We also tend to see a U-shaped relationship between stress and performance – some stress helps motivate behaviour, but too much stress becomes detrimental.

Notably, people vary considerably in the amount of objective and subjective stress experienced, how events are perceived, and their coping ability.

The same objective event might be perceived as an exciting challenge for one person and detrimentally stressful for another. Personality, social factors, available coping strategies, and the social environment all have an impact.

A growing number of secondary students report high levels of distress. Some students have good reason to feel distressed – such as those who have experienced severe traumas or come from unsafe homes and neighbourhoods. Their world is a threatening place, and their physiological systems are constantly on guard. For such students, it becomes important to establish a safe environment and restore basic physiological functioning (Brunzell, Stokes, & Waters, 2016).

But others report being extremely distressed by stressors that ought to manageable. Perceptions might be wrong, or they might not have the right coping skills. For such students, understanding that there are different types of stress and identifying adaptive ways to cope can turn what may seem insurmountable into something more manageable. This activity helps students better understand what stress, is, recognise that stress is not always a bad thing, and start to consider adaptive ways to reframe distress.

Instructions

Place a chair or board at one end of the room with a sign that says "Low Stress" and another chair or board at the other end of the room with a sign that says "High Stress". Ask students to stand where they feel their current stress levels are. If working with an individual student, take a sheet of paper, write "low stress" on the far left of the page, "high stress" to the far-left side of the page, and have them mark with an "X" how they currently feel. Add your own mark to the page.

Next, invite students to share with those standing near them why they placed themselves in the position they chose. What makes them feel high or low on the stress scale? Are their perceptions similar or different? With an individual student, ask the student to explain their mark in relation to where it is positioned.

Bring the students back together for reflection and discussion. Discuss the following points:

1   Stress is variable. Stress can also change constantly throughout the day. It is never permanent.
2   People experience stress differently. What is stressful to one person may not be stressful to others (They might have noticed this in sharing with each other – one person might have been stressed about small things; another might report the same level of stress for something much bigger). Note that their perceptions are very real – we all think differently and uniquely – it's important not to discount a student who feels very stressed about little things.
3   Discuss eustress and distress and describe the U-shape relationship between stress and behaviour. Note that not all stress is bad – we can feel pressure

from good things. And some stress is useful. Stress helps with motivation and preparation. It helps us to get up and go in the morning. But too much stress can be unproductive and we want to catch distress early before it becomes a problem.

4   Ask what students do to manage stress. This is a good opportunity for sharing strategies. For those that rate stress low, ask them what strategies work for them? What keeps their stress low? For those that rate stress high, ask how they have managed stress in the past. Was it successful? And from the successful strategies, what would you be willing to try again.

Activity 2: Celebrity idol

Purpose: To help students recognise their self-talk and to encourage positive self-talk.

Materials: None.

Suggested time for completion: 20–30 minutes.

Introduction

One of the golden rules of life is to "treat others as you would like to be treated". Through childhood and adolescence, parents, teachers, and others help children to learn to be respectful and kind to other people. Most people learn these lessons well. But we don't always follow that same advice for ourselves. At times, perhaps the advice should be "treat yourself as you treat others".

Imagine that you have to do a stressful task. Maybe it's giving a presentation, completing an assignment for a class, or taking a test. What thoughts run through your head? Are they encouraging and full of competence, or do you worry about failing, letting others down, and other negative thoughts? These thoughts are self-talk – the messages we say to ourselves, often at a subconscious level.

Often, we say things to ourselves that we would never dream of saying to someone else. Of course, some negative thoughts are not a bad thing. They can help us not be overly confident and motivate us to work hard. But other times such negative thoughts can become quite toxic, especially when you ruminate (think about the negative thought over and over). In such cases, intervention with a psychologist may be necessary.

An important part of managing one's mental health is to be aware of and be able to take control over our thoughts. If we can recognise that negative thoughts are starting to weigh us down and shift our attention in positive ways, it can stop the rumination before it becomes a problem. This activity helps students recognise their inner voice and shift their thinking in positive ways.

Instructions

Begin by explaining to students that everybody has an inner voice. Psychologists call this voice self-talk. Ask them to spend a minute thinking about their self-talk (alternatively, give students several minutes to free-write any thoughts running through their head, and then note that their writing reflects self-talk).

Next, explain that our self-talk can sometimes be critical. In fact, we can say things to ourselves that we wouldn't dream of saying to another person. Ask students to identify some phrases that they may say to themselves when they self-talk that might not be that helpful or nice. Share one or two of your examples.

Ask students if they would say the phrases they identified to other people. Most of the students will say, "no". Ask them why not? Look for answers along the lines of "that would be mean" or "that would be bullying".

Next, ask what teachers, parents and other friends would think or do if they overheard you speaking like this to someone else. Look for answers along the lines, "they would be disappointed/shocked/appalled" or "they may not want to be my friend". Affirm and validate their answers. Emphasise that negative self-talk can be toxic and unkind and that if we would not say it to someone else, we should not be speaking to ourselves this way.

Next, ask the students to pick an idol – someone they really admire, such as a mentor, a celebrity, a pop or rock star, an artist, a scientist, or another notable person. Invite students to close their eyes and imagine what it would be like if their idol came to their house to visit. What would they say to them? What they would you do with them? Give students several minutes to reflect.

Have students turn to a partner and describe their dream visit with their idol.

Bring the students back together. Invite students to imagine that as they chat with their idol, their idol suddenly reveals that they are feeling worthless, stupid, and unmotivated. In fact, they think they will never accomplish anything.

Returning to work with their partner, invite students to brainstorm:

- What advice would you give your idol?
- What would you say in response to the negative things your idol has said about themselves?
- What help could you steer your idol towards?

Bring students back together for final discussion. Ask some partners to share the advice they came up with. End by telling students to remember treat yourself as good as you would treat your idol.

Activity 3: Group life

> *Purpose*: To help students recognise and value the groups they are a part of or consider strategies for becoming more connected to existing groups for those who feel disconnected.

Materials: *Group life* worksheet (printable handouts available at X https://www.routledge.com/9781138305083).

Suggested time for completion: 20–30 minutes.

Introduction

The groups that we are a part of have a strong influence on our feelings of connection, sense of identity, and mental health. Humans naturally affiliate with others that are similar, they look for things in common such as, living nearby, having shared interests, having the same ethnic or cultural background, or a host of other reasons. Some groups are formal, such as sports teams and clubs, whereas others are informal and less stable, such as various social groups that adolescents might be a part of.

Groups can also have a variety of negative effects. Those who are part of the group (the in-group) feel connected, while those on the outside can feel excluded and rejected. Conflict can occur between different groups. We can feel torn between different groups, trying to balance competing demands and interests. And some groups can be quite harmful to the adolescent or others (e.g., a social group that leads them to smoke, drink, and skip class).

Fostering connection with healthy, supportive groups can help support student belonging and wellbeing. This activity helps students consider the different groups that they are a part of – the role they play, and how they can benefit from being a part of different groups. For students belonging to many groups, this activity can help them evaluate the different groups they are involved in, prioritising those that they feel most connected to. And for those students feel disconnected from their groups, this activity may help students identify ways to connect further.

Instructions

Begin by asking students what groups they are involved in and discuss some of the benefits they may feel. Invite students to pair up with a classmate whom they feel comfortable working with, and then work together to complete the *Group life* worksheet (see below; printable handouts available at https://www.routledge.com/9781138305083; each student should fill out their own sheet but working with a partner can help students think through the questions). End the activity by emphasising the importance of groups that may be raised by the students. Reinforce the value of groups to their learning, development, and sense of belonging. Encourage students to actively do what they can to benefit from the groups they are a part of, and/or act to connect with other groups as needed.

If you are working with an individual student, the responses provided create an audit of their group life. Based on their answers, you might like to help them set goals around what groups they could belong to or how they could work towards being more involved in the groups they are already a part of. You can help them to create a plan that can be followed-up in a later session.

Group life

The formal and informal groups that we are a part of can have a positive or negative influence on our thoughts, feelings, and behaviours. We benefit from being an active group member, allowing the group to meet our needs, and we do what we can to contribute to the group experience for others.

Take a moment and consider the groups you are a part of. Select three groups that you feel most connected to and answer the questions for each group.

Group 1: _____

What is your role in the group?

How does this group impact your thoughts, feelings, and behaviours?

What can you do to contribute more to the group?

What can you do to benefit more from this group?

Group 2: _____

What is your role in the group?

How does this group impact your thoughts, feelings, and behaviours?

What can you do to contribute more to the group?

What can you do to benefit more from this group?

Group 3: _____

What is your role in the group?

How does this group impact your thoughts, feelings, and behaviours?

What can you do to contribute more to the group?

What can you do to benefit more from this group?

Now, consider if there are any groups that you would like to be a part of, or would like to connect with more.

Group: _____

Why do you want to be a part of this group?

What are obstacles to becoming a part of (or connecting better with) this group?

What steps can you take to become a part of (or connect better with) this group?

Group: _____

Why do you want to be a part of this group?

What are obstacles to becoming a part of (or connecting better with) this group?

What steps can you take to become a part of (or connect better with) this group?

Note any other thoughts or reflections here.

Activity 4: Ways of coping

Purpose: To identify and evaluate different coping strategies.

Materials: *Ways of coping* cards (printable handouts available at https://www.routledge.com/9781138305083, cut cards apart before use, with one set of cards per group).

Suggested time for completion: 30–60 minutes.

Introduction

What do you when you face a problem or challenge? Do you seek support, avoid the problem, distract yourself, or use another approach? Our way of dealing with things reflect various coping strategies. Just like how we have our own unique likes, dislikes and interests, coping styles vary for different people – a strategy that works well for one person, may not work for another. The usefulness of the coping strategy is also situation-specific. Still, while strategies are not good or bad per se, some are more productive or healthy than others for different situations (Frydenberg, 2017). For instance, if you are worried about an exam, then dealing with the stress by avoiding studying and playing games all day is not useful, whereas getting help from others would be more adaptive. But when things are totally out of your control, then distracting yourself could be helpful.

This activity helps students think about their regular coping strategies, considering when different strategies may or may not be useful. The strategies emerge from over three decades of work by Professor Erica Frydenberg (2017) and can be a helpful for understanding how a student copes with challenges. The findings from this activity can help students move toward using or improving healthy and adaptive approaches to coping.

Instructions

Begin by asking students to share some of the ways they cope with problems they encounter. Highlight that we each have different ways we typically deal with challenges and problems and might use different strategies for different situations. Sometimes these can be more helpful than others. Invite students to share a few examples of coping well with a problem versus something they did that was unhelpful. Consider sharing one or two personal examples.

Have students form groups of three to five. Invite them to consider a situation (e.g., an upcoming exam that you are worried about) and order the cards from the most helpful to least helpful strategy. Select another situation and repeat. You might have students come up with different situations, or suggest some of the following:

* an upcoming exam that you are worried about
* a friend doesn't invite you to a party

- your team loses a big game
- you oversleep and miss the bus to school
- someone makes fun of another student on social media
- you overhear some boys calling another boy gay in a mean way
- your mum won't allow you to go out with your friends
- you don't understand what you need to do on an assignment
- you have a falling out with your best friend
- your dog runs away
- you lose your telephone
- you forget to watch your favourite TV show
- your mum cooks your least favourite food for dinner
- you want to sleep in but need to wake up early for your sport's team
- you fail an exam.

Bring students back together and consider what strategies generally are more useful and which are less useful. Encourage them to reflect on their typical coping strategy, and to consider whether some of the other strategies might be useful alternatives.

Ways of coping cards

Seek support *Talking about your concerns with friends or others*	Avoid *Avoid the problem to forget about the problem. Withdraw from others. Read, do art, play video games, etc.*	Problem solve *Using a problem-solving approach to dealing with the problem. Evaluating what options can be taken and choosing one based on the best outcomes*
Use Humour *Using humour as a distraction*	Work hard *Concentrate on work as a way to distract thinking about your problem*	Give up *Not try to cope or engage in solving the problem*
Relax *Using relaxation strategies like having a hot bath, or meditation to cope with stress*	Pray *Use religion and belief to pray to God or a higher means for help*	Cry *Crying as way to deal with the issue*
Physical Exercise *Engaging in sports, or exercise*	Wish *Wish for change or that things were different*	Reduce tension *Making yourself feel better by reducing tension in an unhelpful way (e.g., yelling at people, being angry and reckless)*
Talk to a professional *Discuss your concerns with a school psychologist, counsellor, or GP*	Blame self *Blame yourself for the problem that may have occurred*	Take up social action *Creating a survey, joining a protest, or drawing from broader resources to seek a solution to the issue.*
Worry *Worry about your stressors and take no other action*	Think positive *Thinking about the situation in a rational and positive way rather than focusing on the negative*	Accept your best efforts *Acknowledging that somethings are in your control and somethings aren't. Accepting you have done your best.*

Activity 5: The positive mood diary

> *Purpose*: To help students identify times during their day when they experience good moods.
>
> *Materials*: *Positive mood diary* worksheet (printable handouts available at https://www.routledge.com/9781138305083).
>
> *Suggested time for completion*: 5–10 minutes in a group or class, plus 5-minute daily reflection for students across the week.

Introduction

Students experience a range of moods during the day and week, ranging from very positive to very negative. In our study (Allen et al., 2018), we found that positive emotions strongly correlated with school belonging. When you belong, it's easier to feel happy, but it's also easier for others to connect with someone who is happy and positive as opposed to someone that is always miserable.

We also tend to have a negativity bias – we can be prone to remembering negative moods, experiences, and interactions more than we remember positive ones. This means that a young person can have a pretty good day, but then a boring class, a mean text message, or other negative experiences can dominate their perspective on the day.

It can be useful to purposely reflect on positive moods, to recognise when they happen and to analyse the associated thoughts and behaviour. A greater understanding of what makes us happy, as well as the associated cognitions, may allow us to find ways to encourage more positive affect in the future. This activity encourages students to do just that. Our focus here is to analyse the best moods experienced during the day.

Note. This activity specifically focuses on positive moods, rather than identifying a range of moods. Students struggling with clinical needs or mood dysregulation might find it impossible to identify positive moods, such that care should be taken. If concerns are detected during the activity, students should be referred to an appropriate person for support.

Instructions

Invite students to complete the mood diary, aiming for one entry per day over the course of the week. Encourage them to try to hunt for positive moods, even if it seems like a pretty rotten day.

After the week, have students reflect on the experience. What did they notice? What's it like to focus on your positive moods? Were they able to bring about more positive moods?

This activity could be used if working with an individual with minimal adaption.

End with discussing the impact that our moods have on how we function and feel. Also remind students that at times, even despite our best efforts, we can still have really unhappy days – and that's OK. High and low moods are a part of life.

The positive mood diary

How often are you in a positive or negative mood? Studies find that we tend to focus more on our negative moods and experiences than with what goes right. It's helpful to recognise our positive experiences. This can help us remember good times and purposely bring more positive experiences about.

Your task: For the next week, complete this diary at the end of each day. Can you increase your positive moods over the week?

Day 1:
Describe your best mood of the day:
What were you doing when you experienced this mood?
What were you thinking at the time?
How could you make this happen more frequently?

Day 2:

Describe your best mood of the day:

What were you doing when you experienced this mood?

What were you thinking at the time?

How could you make this happen more frequently?

Day 3:

Describe your best mood of the day:

What were you doing when you experienced this mood?

What were you thinking at the time?

How could you make this happen more frequently?

Day 4:

Describe your best mood of the day:

What were you doing when you experienced this mood?

What were you thinking at the time?

How could you make this happen more frequently?

Day 5:

Describe your best mood of the day:

What were you doing when you experienced this mood?

What were you thinking at the time?

How could you make this happen more frequently?

Day 6:

Describe your best mood of the day:

What were you doing when you experienced this mood?

What were you thinking at the time?

How could you make this happen more frequently?

Day 7:

Describe your best mood of the day:

What were you doing when you experienced this mood?

What were you thinking at the time?

How could you make this happen more frequently?

Activity 6: Thought snowballs

Purpose: To identify troubles and worries and provide a fun, visual way to let those troubles go.

Materials: Pen and paper (half-size sheets, at least ten per student).

Suggested time for completion: 20–30 minutes.

Introduction

Professor Barbara Fredrickson (2001) suggests that positive and negative emotions can have opposite effects on our thinking. Negative emotions can narrow our thinking to focus on things that make us worried, sad, angry, et cetera. In contrast, positive emotions can broaden our thinking, help us focus on the world around us, spur on optimism and creativity, and encourage engagement in everyday life.

For many students, school brings various concerns and worries, ranging from trying to complete an assignment on time or earn a certain mark to a variety of social concerns. It's hard to stay focussed on studies when negative thoughts dominate your thinking. Think about the times that you feel really stressed. What does your mind focus on? Often, we think about how stressed we are, or worry about all the things that need to get done. We can even spend more time worrying about getting things done than the time it would have taken to just do what we were worrying about!

Negative emotions are important. They can be an indicator of when things are not right and are a natural reaction to challenges that occur in and around us. But the problem occurs when we hold on to the negative emotions and ruminate on the things that make us feel bad. We need to be able to feel negative emotions, but not get stuck on them.

One way to help manage negative emotions is to recognise the emotions that we feel, then choose to let them go. This activity is a fun way to help students metaphorically throw away their worries and stressors. Obviously, it won't fix all negative emotions (often it's not easy to just throw away our worries), but it can help students think about ways to let go of things weighing them down. The activity ends with inviting students to think about proactive ways to cope with the worries and stressor they have identified.

Instructions

Provide students with half sheets of paper, at least ten pages per person. Instruct students to think about the worries that they have. These might be very small worries or very big worries. Invite students to write down one worry per sheet. If working with a group or class, you might like to emphasise that their worry will not be identified, but if they are concerned about their anonymity, then they should stick to general, non-identifying information. Give students 5–10 minutes to work individually.

Next, ask students about ways they tend to deal with their troubles and worries. Students will provide various answers, such as ignore it, talk to a friend, play an online game, or cry, et cetera. Identify with the students the more adaptive strategies, emphasising that once a worry is managed, they can then let it go and move beyond it. That might mean facing the worry directly, or recognising there is nothing you can do about it – and then letting those worries go.

Now the fun begins. Remind students that they have a handful of worries on their sheets of paper. Ask students to scrunch up their paper into individual balls to make "snow balls". Ask the group – what do you do with snowballs? Hopefully they'll answer "throw them". It's especially fun when it's a snowball fight. And that's what you'll do here. Have a snowball fight, inviting students to pretend their worries are snow balls and they are throwing them away.

Alternatively (or if working with an individual student), scrunch up the paper and play a paper/waste basket type game. You can even introduce fans, and other obstacles to make it more novel.

Bring the students together. Pick up some of the snowballs, open them up, and reveal the worry (have discretion – skip any that should not be shared with the whole group or might identify a specific student). For each one, brainstorm with the group some ways to tackle the worry. Does it need a problem-solving approach? Is it something the young person just needs to cope with? What are some useful coping strategies? Do they need to challenge their thinking around the problem?

Last, throw away the problems. Invite students to gather up any snowballs around them and pitch in the rubbish. End by noting that once problems have been dealt with, we can truly get rid of them!

Activity 7: Helping hands

> *Purpose*: To help students identify where they can go when they need support or help.
>
> *Materials*: Pen and paper.
>
> *Suggested time for completion*: 15–20 minutes.

Introduction

A common challenge for adolescents is not knowing where to go for help and support for themselves or friends. This activity helps students to identify their own personal help-seeking resources. It was originally developed for primary school students, but can bring a smile to the face of older students.

Instructions

Begin with a discussion around help seeking. Ask students where they go when they need help and support – for them or a peer. Suggest several situations and ask for several possibilities. You might want to remind them that different people may have different strengths. One person might be more helpful for practical help like homework, another person might be more helpful for fun help – like making them laugh. Another person might be better for personal support.

Next, ask students to take out a blank sheet of paper (or provide blank paper, one for each student). Instruct them to trace around their hand in the middle of a blank sheet of paper, and then list five people at school they can seek help from when needed – one in each finger.

Next, have students flip the paper over and again trace their hand. List five people outside of school they could seek help from. This list can include resources and local agencies in the local neighbourhood. You could also include professional support in this list as well. In the space outside of the fingers, list ideas on:

• Why is this person helpful?
• What sort of problems could this person help with?

End by emphasising that we don't need to do things all by ourselves. Encourage students to consider reaching out to the helping hands around them when they need it – and to provide a helping hand to others too.

Activity 8: A letter to me

Purpose: To help students gain perspective on their problems.

Materials: None.

Suggested time for completion: 20–30 minutes.

Introduction

Do you ever think back to when you were younger, and think "I wish I knew then what I knew now"? As we get older, we can look back on prior experiences and look at them in perspective. We see the bigger picture of how they fit into our life story. Adolescents are learning how to place things in perspective, but easily get caught up in the day-to-day. Their problems can often seem trivial to us, but to them, it's a big deal.

This activity challenges students to step back and gain perspective on their problems. Yes, it's a big deal now, but in a year from now, or ten years from now, will it really matter?

While many students can benefit from this, there may be some students who are indeed dealing with very big life concerns. For instance, the death of someone close, parental divorce, physical or mental illness, and other major life stressors probably will impact them and have an ongoing effect. It's important to validate these concerns and make sure they get the support they need. This activity is targeted at minor concerns that are *perceived* to be big issues, not to make light of the big concerns.

Instructions

Begin by asking students to close their eyes and imagine that they are now 30 years old. Imagine what they look like, what they are wearing, how they dress, what they do for work, where they live, what their family looks like. Give them a few minutes to imagine the scene.

Next, have them consider a few of their current problems and concerns. Things that are worrying them or tend to get them down – they could be big or small. Ask them to think about what their 30-year-old self may say to them. What advice would they give? What light could they shed? What thoughts would they share on any worries or concerns they may have. Have them write a letter of advice to themselves.

End by emphasising that often when we are caught up in problems and concerns, we lose perspective – little things take all our attention, when in the big picture they really don't matter. That's when we need to regain perspective – and this provides a way to do just that.

Module wrap up: Suggested questions for personal reflection or discussion

1   What will you do differently or continue to do in terms of the way you cope with problems or manage stress?
2   Self-care and self-support are important for wellbeing. What ways will you focus on being kinder to yourself?
3   Seeking help and support are an important way to stay mentally healthy and belong. What are some resources you will try next time you need support?

Final thoughts

This module has touched on some preventative and proactive strategies for supporting the mental health and wellbeing of young people. It encourages students to consider how they cope with issues, where they can go for help, and ways to place problems and concerns in perspective. We note, however, that the module is not designed to be used as the sole intervention tool for students with serious mental health issues. In such cases, providing students with additional support and referral to the school psychologist or external professionals is important.

As part of this, schools should make it clear what supports are available and how teachers should refer cases. Dealing with mental health issues can be a major challenge for teachers, especially when they may feel they have not received sufficient training in these matters. Professional development, clear protocols, and finding ways to support teachers and other staff members is important, especially as they act as a first line of defence for at-risk students.

References

Allen, K., Kern, P., Vella-Brodrick, D., & Hattie, J. & Waters, L., (2018). What schools need to know about belonging: A meta-analysis. *Educational Psychology Review, 30*(1), 1–34.

Allen, K. & McKenzie, V. (2015). Adolescent mental health in an Australian context and future interventions. *Special Issue on Mental Health in Australia for the International Journal of Mental Health, 44*, 80–93. doi: 10.1080/00207411.2015

Anderman, E. M. (2002). School effects on psychological outcomes during adolescence. *Journal of Educational Psychology, 94*(4), 795–809.

Brunzell, T. Stokes, H., & Waters, L. (2016). Trauma-informed positive education: Using positive psychology to strengthen vulnerable students. *Contemporary School Psychology, 20*, 63–83.

Cannon, W. B. (1932). *Wisdom of the body.* New York: W. W. Norton.

Fredrickson, B. L. 2001 The role of positive emotions in positive psychology: the broaden-and-build theory of positive emotions *Am. Psychol, 56*, 218–226.

Friedman, H. S., & Kern, M. L. (2012). Psychological predictors of heart disease. In V. S. Ramachandran (Editor-in-Chief) *Encyclopedia of human behavior*, 2nd Ed. San Diego, CA: Elsevier.

Frydenberg, E. (2017) *Coping and the challenge of resilience.* New York: Palgrave Macmillan.

Keating, D. (2017, April). Stress really is killing us. *CNN website* [opinion piece]. Retrieved from https://edition.cnn.com/2017/04/02/opinions/stress-killing-us-keating-opinion/index.html

Kemeny, M. E. (2007). Psychoneuroimmunology. In H. S. Friedman & R. C. Silver (Eds), *Foundations of health psychology* (pp. 92–116). New York: Oxford University Press.

Kessler, R. C., & Bromet, E. J. (2013). The epidemiology of depression across cultures. *Annual Review of Public Health, 34*, 119–138.

Kia-Keating, M., & Ellis, B. (2007). Belonging and connection to school in resettlement: Young refugees, school belonging, and psychosocial adjustment. *Clinical Child Psychology and Psychiatry, 12*(1), 29–43.

McEwen, B. S. (2006). Protective and damaging effects of stress mediators: Central role of the brain. *Dialogues in Clinical Neuroscience, 8*, 283–293.

McMahon, S., Parnes, A., Keys, C., & Viola, J. (2008). School belonging among low-income urban youth with disabilities: Testing a theoretical model. *Psychology in the Schools, 45*(5), 387–401.

Segerstrom, S. C., & Miller, G. E. (2004). Psychological stress and the human immune system: a meta-analytic study of 30 years of inquiry. *Psychological Bulletin, 104*, 601–630.

Shochet, I. M., Dadds, M. R., Ham, D., & Montague, R. (2006). School connectedness is an underemphasized parameter in adolescent mental health: Results of a community prediction study. *Journal of Clinical Child and Adolescent Psychology, 35*(2), 170–179.

Shochet, I. M., Smyth, T. L., & Homel, R. (2007). The impact of parental attachment on adolescent perception of the school environment and school connectedness. *Australian and New Zealand Journal of Family Therapy, 28*(2), 109–118.

White, M. A., & Kern, M. L., (2018). Positive education: Learning and teaching for wellbeing and academic mastery. *International Journal of Wellbeing, 8*(1), 1–17. doi: 10.5502/ijw.v8i1.588.

Conclusion

Becoming a belonger

We all desire to belong. Whether it's with family, friends, a group, school, work, our community, or other areas, we have a deep need for connection. As adolescents develop a sense of identity, explore who they are and how they fit into the world, a sense of school belonging can provide stability – it supports school performance and mental health – helping them to feel good and function well.

Students who feel disconnected may present for help in a variety of ways. They may want to leave school. They may not see the value in education. They may struggle with making and keeping friendships. They may feel overlooked by their friends. They may have a high level of conflict at home. Their parents may threaten to withdraw them from school. They may believe their teachers do not like them, or that their teachers are choosing favourites that are not them. They may be experiencing mental health concerns such as depression or anxiety. They may not know how to seek help. They may feel lonely or isolated.

While students may be observed by teachers to have friends around them and seem happy, many students still experience a pervading sense of not belonging. For the individual student, these feelings are very real. And while studies find that loneliness does not relate to the number of friends you have around you, the same can be true for a sense of belonging – it's not about the number of relationships around us, but the quality and perception of those relationships that matters more.

School belonging is important for a student's wholistic development at school. Throughout this book, we have focused on addressing school belonging at the individual level, but this is just the beginning. Schools should invest time in assessing their students for a sense of school belonging and using that data to intervene at a whole school level – such interventions benefit all students and not just those who report feeling disconnected (see Allen, Vella-Brodrick, & Waters, 2016). Schools should invest time in ensuring school belonging is a priority. Are there policies in place to manage student disconnection? Is school belonging or building community prioritised in school vision and mission statements? Do teachers and staff have adequate training and professional development to manage school belonging? Is it clear where to go for help and support? Are parents actively involved in the school? Does the school offer peer support programs? Is there a clear focus on school wide practices concerned with mental health promotion? These are some examples of where school belonging can be targeted at other levels within the school system.

Peers, parents, and teachers can all be culpable in contributing to a student feeling like they don't belong. But students can also be flawed in their thinking. They may feel left out, but they also make little effort to change. They *perceive* they are isolated, but don't *take responsibility* to create change. In this book, we have sought to provide practical strategies that teachers, school staff, and practitioners can use with adolescents to help empower them to become *belongers*. Yes, we need to create environments that are supportive and foster connection, but we also need to help young people successfully navigate the challenges they face and take control of their own mental health.

The six modules within this book are packed with activities to help students develop a sense of belonging. The focus areas of the modules are identified in the literature as being significant and important factors associated with boosting belonging (Allen, Kern, Vella-Brodrick, Hattie, and Waters, 2018), while the strategies are derived from a variety of sources. Belonging matters to young people and a construct that is so essential to long term outcomes concerned with psychosocial adjustment, social functioning and mental health it cannot be ignored. This book provides a resource for practitioners and school staff to create a culture of belonging so that all young people can have greater opportunities to become happy and successful citizens in our society.

The literature has widely established with convincing evidence that school belonging is good for students for a variety of factors including academic outcomes, wellbeing and mental health, but less is known about what that practically looks like. We have endeavoured to help fill this gap, in a practical, accessible manner. Finding ways to help young people feel a sense of belonging is an ongoing journey – for the students and all who work with them. We invite you to join us on that journey, contributing your own insights and ideas. Together we can help our young people become belongers.

References

Allen, K., Kern, P., Vella-Brodrick, D., & Hattie, J. & Waters, L., (2018). What schools need to know about belonging: A meta-analysis. *Educational Psychology Review, 30*(1), 1–34. doi: 10.1007/s10648-016-9389-8

Allen, K., Vella-Brodrick, D., & Waters, L. (2016). Fostering school belonging in secondary schools using a socio-ecological framework. *The Educational and Developmental Psychologist, 33*(1), 97–121. doi: 10.1017/edp.2016.5

Further reading

Allen, K.A. & Boyle, C. (Eds) (2018). *Pathways to belonging.* Leiden: Brill Sense.

Allen, K., & Kern, M. L. (2017). *School belonging in adolescents: Theory, research, and practice.* Singapore: Springer Social Sciences.

Brown, B. (2017). *Braving the wilderness: The quest for true belonging and the courage to stand alone.* New York: Random House.

Cacioppo, J. T. & Patrick, W. (2009). *Loneliness: Human nature and the need for social connection.* New York: W. W. Norton & Company.

Cruwys, T., Haslam, A., & Jetten, J. (2018). *The new psychology of health.* Abingdon: Routledge.

Frydenberg, E. (1997). *Adolescent coping: Theoretical and research perspectives.* London: Psychology Press.

Frydenberg, E., Deans, J., O'Brien, K. (2012). *Developing everyday coping skills in the early years.* London: Continuum.

Godin, S. (2011). *We are all weird.* New York: The Domino Project.

Harari, Y. N. (2015). *Sapiens: A brief history of humankind.* New York: Harper.

Holmes, K. (2018). *Mismatch: How inclusion shapes design (simplicity: design, technology, business, life).* Cambridge, MA: The MIT Press.

Jarvis, P. (2009). *Learning to be a person in society.* London: Routledge.

Lieberman, M. D. (2013). *Social: Why our brains are wired to connect.* New York: Crown.

Mackay, H. (2014). *The art of belonging.* Sidney: Macmillan Australia.

Paley, V. G. (1993). *You can't say you can't play.* Cambridge, MA: Harvard UP.

Paley, V. G. (2000). *The kindness of children.* Cambridge, MA: Harvard UP.

Parker, P. (2018). *The art of gathering: How we meet and why it matters.* New York: Riverhead Books.

Putnam, R. D. (2001). *Bowling alone: The collapse and revival of American community* (1st ed). New York: Simon and Schuster.

Riesman, D., Glazer, N., & Denney, R. (2001). *The lonely crowd* (Abridged and Revised ed). New Haven, CT: Yale UP.

Riley, K. (2013). *Leadership of place: Stories from schools in the US, UK and South Africa.* London: Bloomsbury.

Riley, K. (2017). *Place, belonging and school leadership: Researching to make the difference.* London: Bloomsbury.

Rowe, F. & Stewart, D. E. (2010). *Promoting school connectedness: Using a whole-school approach.* Saarbrucken: LAP Lambert.

Sales, L. (2018). *Any ordinary day.* Australia: Penguin Random House Australia.

Street, H. (2018). *Contextual wellbeing: Creating positive schools from the inside out.* Subiaco, Australia: Wise Solutions.

Svendsen, G. T. (2014). *Trust.* Aarhus: Aarhus UP.

Turkle, S. (2012). *Alone together: Why we expect more from technology and less from each other.* New York: Basic Books.

Waters, L. (2017). *The strength switch: How the new science of strength-based parenting can help your child and your teen to flourish.* New York: Avery.

Glossary

Academic motivation Academic motivation is a student's drive to be engage in their learning at school. It may involve the ability to plan, set goals, and exhibit academic confidence and resilience.

Individual needs Individual needs refer to the unique needs and differences of all students that when addressed provide equitable access to educational opportunities.

Mental health promotion A proactive approach to fostering wellbeing and minimising the experience of mental illness.

Meta-analysis A quantitative method of summarising research studies. A thorough search of existing studies is done, and the findings are statistically combined to indicate how much different variables relate to each other (e.g., school belonging and mental health), as well as other factors that affect those relationships (e.g., gender, type of study done).

Parent support The ability for parents and primary caretakers to provide academic support as well as social support, open communication, supportive behaviours (e.g., giving encouragement, gratitude), and show care and compassion towards their children.

Peer support The trust and closeness exhibited by friends and peers. Supportive peers offer social as well as academic encouragement.

School belonging A student's sense of affiliation to his or her school – one's feeling of being connected to a school within a school social system.

Teacher support Teacher support is the academic and social support shown by teachers. It involves teachers showing students mutual respect, care, encouragement, friendliness, autonomy, and fairness.

About the authors

Dr Kelly-Ann Allen is nationally and internationally recognised as a researcher and practitioner in the field of school belonging. She is the inaugural director and founder of the International Belonging Research Laboratory, which represents a large group of belonging researchers and leaders from around the world. She regularly presents her work at national and international conferences as scientific papers, workshops, and invited keynote addresses and symposiums. Dr Allen frequently interacts with the media through general publications, interviews, and podcasts that contribute to the broader reach and impact of her work. Dr Kelly Allen's PhD, which studied how school belonging could be increased in students in secondary schools, was awarded the Australian Psychological Society's 2016 "Award for Excellent PhD Thesis in Psychology" and the 2016 Psychology of Relationships Interest Group's "Psychology of Relationships Thesis Award".

Kelly-Ann is a fellow of the College of Educational and Developmental Psychologists, where she is also Treasurer for the National committee. She is a committee member for the American Psychological Society, Division 15 (Education Psychology) and associate editor for three journals: *Australian Journal of Psychology* (Wiley), *The Educational and Developmental Psychologist* (Cambridge University Press) and *Australian Community Psychologist*. Kelly-Ann also serves on several editorial boards, including The British Psychological Society's, Child and Educational Psychologist and Social Health and Behaviour.

Kelly-Ann is a board director for both The Homeless Project Ltd and Early Childhood Intervention Australia (ECIA) (Victoria, Tasmania), a peak body for early childhood intervention in Australia. Her activities focused on community engagement have won awards including the University of Melbourne's Peter McPhee Award for student engagement and the Leader's in Community Award.

Dr Allen's interest in belonging has seen her publish several chapters and peer-reviewed papers related to school belonging as well as two other books: *School Belonging in Adolescents: Theory, Research, and Practice* (Springer) and *Pathways to Belonging: Contemporary Research in School Belonging* (Brill).

Dr Peggy (Margaret) Kern is an associate professor at the Centre for Positive Psychology within the University of Melbourne's Graduate School of Education. Originally from the United States, she now lives in Australia, and often travels around the world, connecting with different peoples and cultures.

Originally trained in social and personality psychology, she embraces collaboration and interdisciplinary work. Her research draws on multiple fields of inquiry, including health, positive, social, personality, and developmental psychology, public health, education, systems science, and computer science to address the question of thriving across the lifespan. What distinguishes different life trajectories? What does it mean to live well? How can we help people to not only survive life, but to truly thrive? She has spent the past decade systematically unpacking these questions. She incorporates a variety of methodologies into her work, including archival research, meta-analysis, psychometric/ measurement work, big data, language analysis, integrative data analysis, qualitative, and mixed method approaches, resulting in several methodological innovations. She also actively translates her research for organisations and lay audiences, bridging gaps between research and practice through books, talks, and workshops.

Dr Kern also strives to live out a healthy lifestyle. She enjoys being active, including long-distance running, cycling, swimming, and hiking. She won the Charlottesville Marathon in 2008, completed a half Ironman event in 2016, and now simply enjoys staying active and experiencing the world around her.

Appendices

Appendix A: The school belonging scale

School belonging scale

In reviewing the research (Allen, Kern, Vella-Brodrick, Hattie & Waters, 2018), we identified six types of factors that have been found to impact upon school belonging: academic motivation, social and emotional competencies, mental health, teacher support, parent support, and peer support. These six sets of factors inform the modules of this book.

To help identified which modules might be most relevant to the needs of your students, have your students complete the following questions (for an online version or paper handouts, see https://www.routledge.com/9781138305083). Then, use the scoring codes to determine which areas students are doing well at and where they might be struggling. You could also have students complete this again after working through a module, to see if scores improve.

Directions

Read each of the following statements and indicate how well this describes your thoughts, feelings and experiences (not at all, somewhat, or very much).

	Not at all	Somewhat	Very much
Connecting with teachers			
1 I feel connected with my teachers			
2 I get along well with my teachers			
3 My teachers care about me as a person			
4 My teachers care about my learning			
5 I can talk to my teachers about both academic and personal issues			
6 My teachers treat me fairly			
7 I respect my teachers			
8 I feel like my teachers understand who I am as a person			
9 I communicate well with my teachers			
10 I feel close to my teachers			
Connecting with parents/ caregivers			
1 I feel connected with my parent(s)/ caregiver			
2 I get along well with my parents			
3 My parents care about me as a person			

4	My parents care about my learning			
5	I can talk to my parents about both academic and personal issues			
6	My parents treat me fairly			
7	I respect my parents			
8	I feel like my parents understand who I am as a person			
9	I communicate well with my parents			
10	My parents support my learning			
Connection with peers				
1	I feel connected with my peers at my school			
2	I get along well with my peers			
3	My peers care about me as a person			
4	My peers support my learning			
5	I can talk to my peers about both academic and personal issues			
6	My peers are accepting and tolerating of others			
7	I respect my peers			
8	I feel like my peers understand who I am as a person			
9	I communicate well with my peers			
10	I feel close to my peers			

(continued)

(continued)

	Not at all	Somewhat	Very much
Connecting with oneself			
1 I know my strengths and weaknesses			
2 I believe I can do the things I try			
3 I believe things will work out, even if challenging at the time			
4 I understand my thoughts and emotions			
5 I like myself as a person			
6 I understand who I am as a person			
7 I am proud of what I do			
8 I get along well with others			
9 I'm good at managing my emotions			
10 I regularly set and achieve goals			
Connecting with learning			
1 I enjoy learning new things			
2 I am a good student			
3 I am motivated to learn at school			
4 I have high aspirations for my future			
5 I value my classes			
6 I have a regular study routine			
7 I value my school			
8 I feel engaged and interested in my classes			
9 I feel comfortable asking for help with my schoolwork when needed			
10 I embrace failure			

Connecting with help			
1 I effectively deal with stress			
2 I cope well when things go wrong			
3 I feel connected with one or more groups at school			
4 I have numerous ways to deal with problems			
5 I feel comfortable asking for help when needed			
6 I'm generally in a positive mood			
7 I easily let go of worries			
8 I know where to go for help			
9 I rarely feel anxious or depressed			
10 I am kind to myself			

Scoring

Within each category, score the responses as:

Not at all = 0

Somewhat = 1

Very much = 2

Add up the scores for each category

Connecting with teachers: _____   Connecting with parents: _____

Connecting with peers: _____   Connecting with oneself: _____

Connecting with learning: _____   Connecting with help: _____

Scores can range from 0 to 20 in each category. Consider focusing on an area where students score lowest.

Reference

Allen, K. A., Kern, P., Vella-Brodrick, D., Waters, L., & Hattie, J. (2018). What schools need to know about belonging: A meta-analysis. *Educational Psychology Review, 30*(1), 1–34. doi: 10.1007/s10648-016-9389-8

Appendix B: Classroom belonging scale

Introduction

Research has shown that the relationship a student has with their teacher is a powerful predictor of their sense of belonging to school. The *Classroom belonging scale* is designed to measure the student–teacher relationship. The scale was developed by Dr Allen and her colleague, Dr Vicki McKenzie, at the University of Melbourne in 2013. The questions give an indication of students' perception of the quality of their relationship with the teacher. By administering the survey, it also makes a clear statement to the students that the teacher cares about them and wants to work at building a positive relationship.

Instructions

The *Classroom belonging scale* is provided below. Administer the survey to the students in their class. You might consider re-administering the scale each term to assess whether responses have changed over time (printable copies available at https://www.routledge.com/9781138305083).

Introduce the survey using the following script:

> As a teacher, it is important for me to develop a good relationship with my students, helping you to connected to our school. To help me better understand your experiences, I would like to collect some information on how you are getting along in this class. There are nine questions to answer that will help me improve my teaching practices and our classroom environment. Please read each statement carefully and then rate how strongly you agree. There are no right or wrong answers, but it will be most useful to me if you indicate how you honestly feel. I will use your responses to help me improve my own practices to be as supportive as possible.

Classroom belonging scale

Please take a moment and rate how much you agree or disagree with each of the following statements. Please be honest – there are no right or wrong answers.

I have a good relationship with my teacher.

☐ Strongly disagree　☐ Disagree　☐ Neither agree nor disagree　☐ Agree　☐ Strongly agree

My teacher is fair and treats all students in a constructive and positive way.

☐ Strongly disagree　☐ Disagree　☐ Neither agree nor disagree　☐ Agree　☐ Strongly agree

My teacher allows me to have a say and share my ideas and thoughts with my class.

☐ Strongly disagree　☐ Disagree　☐ Neither agree nor disagree　☐ Agree　☐ Strongly agree

My teacher respects me.

☐ Strongly disagree　☐ Disagree　☐ Neither agree nor disagree　☐ Agree　☐ Strongly agree

My teacher expects that I will do well.

☐ Strongly disagree　☐ Disagree　☐ Neither agree nor disagree　☐ Agree　☐ Strongly agree

My teacher is friendly and likeable.

☐ Strongly disagree　☐ Disagree　☐ Neither agree nor disagree　☐ Agree　☐ Strongly agree

My teacher cares for me and is available to listen and support me beyond my schoolwork

☐ Strongly disagree　☐ Disagree　☐ Neither agree nor disagree　☐ Agree　☐ Strongly agree

The work I am doing with my teacher is valuable and helpful for my future goals

☐ Strongly disagree ☐ Disagree ☐ Neither agree nor disagree ☐ Agree ☐ Strongly agree

My teacher is available for help with my work.

☐ Strongly disagree ☐ Disagree ☐ Neither agree nor disagree ☐ Agree ☐ Strongly agree

Making sense of the results

The questions can be considered separately, or the user might calculate an overall belonging score. To do this, the responses are scored as:

1 = strongly disagree

2 = disagree

3 = neither agree nor disagree

4 = agree

5 = strongly agree

Give each question a score, then calculate the mean (add up the numbers and divide by 9). This gives an overall indication of classroom belonging.

After receiving responses, consider spending some time reflecting on how the students responded, both the students as a whole and individuals within the class. How many students agreed or strongly agreed with the questions, and how many disagreed or were uncertain? Are specific students more connected than others? Are there specific questions where scores were especially high or low? How do you feel about the results?

As you consider the strategies in Module 1, you might also consider if there are specific strategies that might be helpful to support students to connect well with you and other teachers, especially if one or two areas are particularly low or concerning. Fortunately, there are a lot of resources available online and around the school that can be helpful. For instance:

- If students rate relationships, likeability, and caring lower, you might consider spending more time working on their rapport with students.
- If fairness and respect are lower, you might want to rethink your disciplinary practices and consider involving students in setting classroom rules, boundaries and consequences.
- If expectations are lower, you might ensure you are clearly articulating what you believe the students can achieve personal success over their learning. It may also be worth discussing school policies, so students are clear early on what the school expectations are.
- If values are lower, you might want to try to make the value of each lesson particularly clear to the students.
- If academic support is lower, it may be worth reflecting on why this could be the case. Is it low due to time pressure? Or unavailability to students outside of class? What support can leadership provide to rectify this issue? Are students encouraged to email questions or questions?

Notes for success

The responses from students should remain confidential and should be used only to develop an understanding of the students' perceptions and for your own self-reflection on your practices. While you may wish to discuss the results with a supervisor, mentor, or colleagues, responses should not be used by school leadership for any other purpose (e.g., performance reviews) than for what it was originally intended. The responses are for teachers' information only, designed to facilitate reflection on the areas that may be maintained or improved.

Although the scale is designed primarily for a group setting with a teacher, it can also be used for an individual session with a student. The student may wish to rate/discuss each item with a counsellor or teacher and talk through each of the points.

For a mental health professional, the student could be asked to give some examples (e.g., can you think of a time when you were not listened to? How did you feel? What could you have done?). The feedback might be kept confidential, or the mental health professional (with the student's permission and within the boundaries of confidentiality) may act as an advocate and share the student's perceptions with a teacher concerned.

The *Classroom belonging scale* is reproduced with permission.

Allen, K-A & McKenzie, V. (2013). The classroom belonging scale. Figshare. Retrieved from: https://figshare.com/articles/Classroom_Belonging_Scale_docx/7042478. doi: 10.6084/m9.figshare.7042478

Index

References in *italics* are to figures and worksheets; those in **bold** to the glossary.

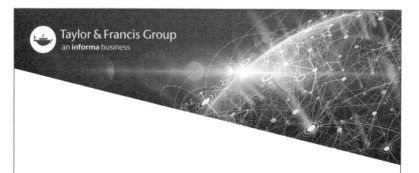